James Fitzpatrick
281 Manse Rd S
West Hill
PO

Reverend William Allan

The Quiet Place

By

The Rev. William Allan

A Short Series of Meditations
Broadcast from the
Rogers Radio Station
C F R B (435 m.—690 k.)
Toronto

Thomas Nelson & Sons, Limited
Toronto

Copyright, Canada
THOMAS NELSON & SONS, LIMITED
1933

Foreword

These morning meditations were suggested by the mood of the moment and arose out of experiences which were enriched by contact with many other minds—so that I am debtor to many who have borne testimony to the goodness of God in the land of the living.

The things of which they speak have been tested in the crucible of my own life—and I can add my word to that of the Psalmist and say, "O taste and see that the Lord is good: blessed is the man that trusteth in Him."

Hundreds of letters from Canada and the United States have assured me that the ministry of the "Morning Devotions" Radio Circle, CFRB, Toronto, each Monday, Wednesday and Friday, has met a real need. And it is in response to a wide-spread desire to have these messages in a more permanent form that this book is being published.

Despite the fact that cold type does not always succeed in carrying the warmth of the human voice the book is sent forth with the hope that it may be a means of blessing and help to all whose eyes scan its pages.

As our Announcer used to say so often when he was introducing us to our radio audience: "Storm-swept skies, and the turmoil of the day, hold no terrors for those who know the secret of the Quiet Place."

Contents

	Page
The Quiet Place	7
What a Night	10
Trials Transformed into Triumphs	13
Meet the Great Physician	17
Babyhood Became a Sacred Thing	20
Does God Care?	24
A Good Investment	28
The Folly of Indecision	31
A Greater than Solomon	35
The Ways of God with Men	37
Journeying toward the Sunrising	42
The Ministry of Affliction	46
Living Life Over Again	50
A Tonic in a Text	54
A Singer and a Song	58
At the Beginning of the Best	61
The Technique of Living	64
Love's Triumphs	68
Wasted Privileges	71
Working Toward Success	73
Wanted—More Reality	78
Devotion to a Purpose	81
The Ministry of the Mountain-Top	84
Meeting the Unexpected	88
Losing One's Ideal	92
Why These Denials?	96
A Startling Question	100
Praying Women	104
Guided by God	108
Sinning and Suffering	112
After a Fortieth Birthday	114
A Mind in Subjection	120
Seeing Jesus	124

The Quiet Place

In times, such as we are passing through now, when the load laid upon us seems too heavy to bear—when our nerves are all frayed, and fear grips our imagination, we are to be congratulated if we have discovered the secret of "The Quiet Place".

In a time of great stress and sore trial in the experience of God's ancient people, the Jews, the prophet Isaiah said by way of instruction and inspiration, "For thus saith the Lord God, the Holy One of Israel; in returning and rest shall ye be saved; in quietness and in confidence shall be your strength." And in another place speaks thus, "Thus saith the Lord, the Holy One of Israel, and his Maker, Ask Me of things to come concerning My sons, and concerning the work of My hands command ye Me."

The Quiet Place is a place of prayer, regarding which Jesus had this to say: "When thou prayest, enter into thy closet, and when thou hast shut thy door, pray to thy Father which is in secret; and thy Father which seeth in secret shall reward thee openly."

It would not be possible to exaggerate the importance of the place, the purpose and the power of prayer in a well-balanced life—whether it be the life of an individual, a congregation, or a nation. The necessity for prayer has never been suspended. It is a Divine decree which dare not be ignored except at the risk of having to meet an incalculable loss! This decree is backed up both by the teaching and the example of Jesus, and by the testimony of a triumphant Church.

Evils within the Church and within the home, as well as in business and in the State, are not new. They are as old as these institutions; and the remedy for them, according to St. Paul, is prayer. He urges this in many an earnest appeal; and he supports his appeal by his own prayer-life.

The twentieth century has found no substitute for prayer; and it is surely a day of substitutes! We have substitutes for almost everything under heaven—and the Church has allowed herself to become infected with the thought that something else can be substituted for the primitive practice of prayer. But she is sadly mistaken! And the sequel is seen in her sorry plight—for at this moment she is but a shadow of her apostolic self.

Jeremiah has something to say which ought to lead us to seek the seclusion of the quiet place to test his statements in our own experience. "Moreover the word of the Lord came unto Jeremiah the second time, while he was yet shut up in the court of the prison, saying, Thus saith the Lord the maker thereof, the Lord that formed it, to establish it; the Lord is his name; Call unto me and I will answer thee, and shew thee great and mighty things, which thou knowest not."

The wrestlings of a simple-hearted faith constitute the mightiest force for God the Church can command.

The Old Testament is full of examples of the truth of this statement. The glory of the upper room at Pentecost lay in the presence of a group of simple-hearted souls who dared to trust where they could not trace. For them, it was enough to know that God had spoken. Their beclouded reason was pleased to bow in the presence of that revelation; and the result was that the place was shaken as there was launched upon society an organization Divinely created and Divinely directed as an ark of safety in the wildest storm that can come upon mankind.

Can my prayer change the purposes of God? This is not just a speculative question; it is intensely practical. Much depends upon the answer. Any doubt on this point will almost be the death of your prayer-life. Is my approach to God in the Quiet Place an errand of real life, or do I simply go through a form of words? Am I only expressing in a pious way some hopeless desires, with no definite object to gain, other than to work myself into a devotional frame of mind? Is this the business in which I am about to engage as I enter The Quiet Place? If that place is to mean to us what God wants it to mean, it ought to be as true of us as it was of a certain great puritan of whom Dr. Chalmers spoke: "His prayers have an intensely business-like spirit."

> "Who may not strive, may yet fulfil
> The harder task of standing still,
> And good but wished, with God is done."

What a Night!

What a wonderful night that must have been when Jesus gathered with His disciples to observe for the last time, the Feast of the Passover. What His thoughts and feelings were, only the Father could understand. Jesus knew that for centuries this Feast had borne eloquent testimony to Himself and to the work of redemption He had come to do. He could see the blindness of mind of those who were leaders of the blind. Into the innermost being of Judas He had looked again and again, as He marvelled at the treachery of a heart that could play the traitor to its best friend! And He prayed for Judas with all the earnestness of which His unique nature was capable.

None new better the weakness of those who were His followers; and yet there never was a heart that held such love for the erring children of men. It is this fact that gives us fresh courage in the hour of our shame—when, overtaken by sin, we despise ourselves and feel that it is no use trying to stem the tide. No one understands us quite like Jesus! No one is so ready to make allowance for the weakness that leads to sin, and none is so quick to forget our failures and inspire us with new hope for the future.

Between the Passover and the Lord's Supper we are told that "Judas went out, *and it was night.*"

Yes, it was night in more senses than one. A darker night than the one that enshrouded the Syrian

What a Night!

sky in blackness had fallen upon the soul of Judas. And it was a night that would never have a morning. The darkness and despair of eternal doom had already settled down upon the soul of one who at one time had evidently given promise of better things. Surely Judas must have had certain gifts and graces else Christ would never have chosen him for the position he occupied in the apostolic group!

"Then said Jesus unto them, All ye shall be offended because of me this night for it is written, I will smite the shepherd, and the sheep of the flock shall be scattered abroad." In these words, Jesus is quoting from the prophet Zechariah; and He endeavours to show them that it is about to be fulfilled in their experience.

What a wonderful book the Bible is; what a light it sheds upon the future; what a message it has for this time of trouble through which the whole world is passing. What a crime against our own souls to be ignorant of its contents! Oh, that it might be sweeter to our taste than the honeycomb, and more precious in our eyes than fine gold!

Can you imagine how they must have felt when the Son of God plainly predicted that they would all forsake Him? When He had told them that one of their number would betray Him, we read that they all said, "Lord, is it I?" But on this occasion silence seems to have fallen upon them all except Peter. Perhaps they were looking into their hearts and asking themselves, "What is there in my make-up that I have not detected which will descend to the depths outlined in this start-

The Quiet Place

ling prediction? Can it be true that I am so destitute of courage and gratitude that I shall yet forsake Him Who is my God, my Saviour, and my Friend?"

"Peter answered and said unto Him, Though all men should be offended because of Thee, yet will I never be offended."

At first sight that statement of faith in himself seems splendid. But when it is examined a little more closely you can easily see that it does not contribute anything to the credit of Peter. In effect he was contradicting Christ, and it is always foolish and dangerous to disagree with Jesus. Whether he knew it or not, his contradiction of Christ was at the same time a condemnation of the other disciples. It illustrated how ignorant we are of our true selves. While we are condemning others we may be far worse ourselves. It is true that the others forsook Jesus, as He said they would,—but Peter did something that deserved greater condemnation when he denied his Lord with oaths and curses! In the light of these things let us be careful to cultivate humility of heart, meekness of spirit, steadfastness of purpose, less confidence in ourselves and a larger confidence in Jesus Christ.

> "The world is a looking glass,
> Wherein ourselves are shown,—
> Kindness for kindness, cheer for cheer,
> Coldness for gloom, repulse for fear,—
> To every soul its own,
> We cannot change the world a whit,
> Only ourselves who look in it."

Trials Transformed into Triumphs

Perhaps one of the best investments we could make to-day would be to take a few minutes out of the day's activities to look at twelve verses which are to be found in St. Matthew, chapter twenty—verses seventeen to twenty-eight.

Jesus is on His way to Jerusalem, and He takes His twelve disciples apart and tells them that He is about to be betrayed and crucified. "Then came to Him the mother of Zebedee's children with her sons, worshipping Him, and desiring a certain thing of Him. But Jesus answered and said, Ye know not what ye ask."

When we read a narrative like this, the trouble with many of us is that, while we may be interested we are not influenced in any practical way. The happenings recorded seem so remote that we fail to relate them to our individual lives. While we are together in this romantic way, give me the privilege, during these few fleeting moments, of trying to correct this.

First of all I would point out that if the record teaches us anything, it teaches that life is not made up of a series of happenings which have little or no relation to each other. *Life is a whole.* And the smallest detail in it plays an important part in the development of the Divine Purpose.

Think of these words which fell from the lips of Jesus: "The very hairs of your head are numbered."

The Quiet Place

"Not a sparrow falleth to the ground without your Father."

Blessed be God, your troubles are reckoned—your tears are numbered! These valleys you often hesitate to enter, and in which you are often chilled to the heart, are of His ordering. Indeed most of them, if not all, are excavated by God's hand.

Bring yourself to see, as others have done, that every cross-current, every contrary wind, every cold biting blast, every steep climb up some mountain-path of difficulty holds its own important place in the Divine Plan for your life!

No test comes to any of us which is not common to all. And with every test God has provided a way of escape.

Hemmed in, as no doubt you often are, by difficulties which fill you with dismay, you may be tempted to make your own way of escape. But God's way is the only honourable way! His ways leads to the larger development of your character, the strengthening of your will, the purifying of your affections, the clarifying of your understanding and the purging of your conscience.

Your life is not like a heap of loose stones unless you yourself make it so. It ought to be a well-built, shapely, stable structure if it is being built according to His Plan.

Why, then, this restlessness Why this feverishness and discontent? "All things work together for good to them that love God." Don't judge the Plan in the light of your own likes and dislikes—judge it in the light of the goodness and wisdom and love of God. When it is complete and you know even as you are known, you will then be able to judge correctly. Till then trust God and go steadily forward. Be so surrendered to the will of God that Jesus will never have occasion to say, "Ye know not what ye ask."

The man who can so deal with his future as Jesus dealt with His can never be driven to despair. He is master of his fate. Tragedies are transformed into triumphs as we come to see that the pains we often have to endure are but the punctuation marks to bring out the sense and beauty of the whole of life's story.

Jesus was never surprised by anything that happened because He was so perfectly in line with the Father's will. Let us seek a similar alignment.

With the shadow of the Cross falling across their pathway you might have expected them to have been awed. But instead of that they are thinking only of themselves and their own gain. They heard His words but understood not His thoughts.

How easy and natural it would have been to have condemned James and John is revealed in the indignation of the ten as recorded in verse twenty-four. How easy it would have been to have lost heart with the twelve! But Christ can redeem the hour of bitterness and transform it into a season of sublime sweetness. He can turn the time of greatest trial into an hour of glorious triumph. His enemies can crucify and bury Him, but He will rise again. The Cross stands not only

The Quiet Place

for an objective of truth, but for a subjective experience and when we enter into the enjoyment of such an experience we have at the same time come into the possession of the power by which all our trials can be transformed into the most glorious triumphs.

> "The happiest heart that ever beat
> Was in some quiet breast,
> That found the common daylight sweet,
> And left to heaven the rest."

Meet the Great Physician

In the fifth chapter of the Gospel according to St. John, we have the story of a man who had been so long in a state of helplessness that, when Jesus met him, he had about reached the point of utter hopelessness.

At the sixth verse we read: "When Jesus saw him lie, and knew that he had been now a long time in that case He saith unto him, Wilt thou be made whole?"

What a difference it makes in the case of any life when Jesus gets a chance to address Himself to that life's need. He presents to us the opportunity to arise out of our helplessness, and dispels the last long shadows of dark despair.

For thirty-eight years this man had known what he wanted to do, and he knew the limbs with which it should be done, but he lacked the power with which to perform. His trouble was a certain kind of paralysis which had held him in its grip through those long years.

We too sometimes suffer from certain kinds of paralysis in the spiritual part of our being. There is the paralysis of *speech*. There are those to whom we feel we should speak about the deepest things of life: of the awful fact of sin, the mystery of the atonement, the glorious possibility of forgiveness as something which must be felt by every life if that life is not to be lost forever amid the wreckage and ruin of the awful consequences of sin. But, when we have tried to speak about such matters, speech has been petrified on our lips—and it may be that another soul has gone to its doom!

Or perhaps there has been conceived within your mind the beautiful form of some unselfish act which, if carried out, might have led to a larger and lovelier life of usefulness, but the vision has vanished only to leave you in the all-embracing grip of your own plans and pleasures. What a shock you might get if you were given now one real glimpse of what you have lost because you are suffering from the paralysis of well-doing!

To us also Jesus comes and says, "Wilt thou be made whole?" *Whole!* What a wonderful word; and what a glorious condition of life it suggests.

When Jesus meets a soul along any of life's highways or byways, and steps across the threshold of that life in all the glory and grace of His healing presence and power, that life is henceforth enabled to obey the noblest impulses and aspirations that pass within the sweep of its vision. Now there is no break between the picture and the performance! The ideal becomes the real — and worth-while ideas are expressed in Christ-like conversation and conduct.

Abraham-like, we are ready, at the call of God, to start early in the morning for the place of sacrifice, confident that, even though it be hid from our eyes, God has some good reason for asking us to do what may seem to be contrary to all human inclination—and every sacrificial act will lead to some larger development of the character and still further expressions of the Divine approval.

To be made whole means that we can now see with what the Bible calls "the single eye". Our consecration is not fitful or feeble, but whole-hearted and steadfast. Now we respond to the cup, however bitter its contents—and to the cross, however cruel its thorns or long its nails, without murmur or complaint.

There is a primary condition which you must meet before the Son of God can work the miracle of healing in your case—He must have the consent of your will.

Your will may be enfeebled, and you may not trust yourself even when you say *yes;* but if you will sincerely say that you are willing to be made willing, His power, through His Word, shall come into operation in your life and the healing work shall come to pass.

Hitherto you have been vacillating in purpose, cowardly in confession, and paralyzed in action—but if you will commit yourself to Christ everything will be changed. Weakness will give place to strength; ignorance will give place to knowledge, fear will give place to courage, selfishness will give place to generosity, fault-finding will give place to praise; and you will become *master* of all that formerly made you a slave.

> "The Great Physician now is near,
>   The sympathizing Jesus!
> He speaks the drooping heart to cheer,
>   Oh, hear the voice of Jesus."

Babyhood Became a Sacred Thing

More than seven hundred years before that birth took place, which we celebrate every year as Christmas comes around, a Hebrew prophet, named Micah, guided by the Spirit of God, looked down the corridor of the centuries and said, "But thou, Bethlehem Ephratah, though thou be little among the thousands of Judah, yet out of thee shall he come forth unto me that is to be a ruler in Israel; whose goings forth have been from of old, from everlasting."

It is not our purpose at present, neither have we the time in this brief meditation to deal with the details of this remarkable revelation, other than to observe how particular this speaker for God is to designate the exact location where the long-looked-for Messiah was to come.

Standing on the pinnacle of prophecy, with the whole world before him, his prophetic eye rests on a little town, six miles south of Jerusalem—and with the confidence of one who had actually been there when it happened and was describing it historically — he announces that in Bethlehem should be born One whose reign would be that of universal and everlasting King.

Bethlehem, little more than a hamlet, was situated on a limestone ridge. It had already earned the right to be considered a place of renown. It was here that

Jacob had laid away in death the remains of his beloved Rachel; and because of the pillar that he erected over her grave it is called the Pillar of Rachel's Tomb to this day. On its emerald-like slopes, that sacred courtship was started which makes the Book of Ruth one of the most charming tales in all literature. Here David was born; and here he shepherded his sheep, a beautiful type of Him of whom Micah was thinking when he uttered the prophecy of our text.

I don't think that Micah's life could ever quite be the same again after God had used his mind and his mouth as the channel through which He would transmit to the children of men the information as to the exact birthplace of His only begotten Son. It is impossible for the creature to come into contact with the Creator in any intimate way without the mind being enlightened, the heart enlarged, and the life enriched.

But every life comes to an end at the entrance to the valley of the shadow of death—even such a life as the prophet's must have been after this incident. But as he steps down into that valley with the memory of this prediction still fresh in his mind, I think I can hear him sing, "I know that my Redeemer liveth, and that He shall stand at the latter day upon the earth."

Then century after century comes and goes to lose itself in the vastness of eternity. And each century carries with it the ruins of many a man-made scheme, and witnesses the downfall of many a proud empire. Again and again during these centuries, Micah's prediction, as it was meditated upon by devout souls, must have seemed to be on the point of dissolving into space. The sceptre has departed from Judah, and the throne of David has crumbled into ruins. Sheep are still to be seen grazing on the hill-sides of Bethlehem, but no Prince of the House of David is to be seen on the horizon of the immediate future. Nevertheless God has spoken regarding a birth that is to take place at Bethlehem, and the problem is, how is this prophecy to be fulfilled? *With God Included Anything Is Possible.*

Oh to feel the pressure of His will upon my will; and to realize that no detail is so insignificant or unimportant to play a part in the carrying forward to a glorious consumation the Kingdom of our Lord and Saviour, Jesus Christ.

Across the Mediterranean, on another continent, in all the imperial splendour of Rome, sits Caesar Agustus. Little does he realize the part he is playing in the carrying out of the Divine Programme! But it is his decree that all the world should be taxed, which sets the wheels in motion to have a marvellous prophecy, again and again endangered during seven centuries, minutely accomplished.

Dead indeed must be that imagination that does not feel in Bethlehem on that first Christmas that *God is here!* It is impossible to stand in the presence of the infant Jesus and resist the conviction that God's purposes are from the beginning, and that nothing can prevent their realization, since in some mysterious way He seems to control every movement of the will of man.

Babyhood Became a Sacred Thing

The birth at Bethlehem consecrated for evermore the cradle of every child, and demonstrated that the presence of Jesus transforms the simplest surroundings into a very vestibule of heaven. Ever since Jesus was born babyhood has been a sacred thing, and infancy can sometimes become a gospel.

> "O little town of Bethlehem,
> How still we see thee lie!
> Above thy deep and dreamless sleep
> The silent stars go by:
> Yet in thy dark streets shineth
> The everlasting Light;
> The hopes and fears of all the years
> Are met in thee to-night."

Does God Care?

My dear friends, I crave the privilege of directing your attention to a portion of the Word of God which, while it deals with something that happened many centuries ago, has a message of great comfort for many who are being sorely tried to-day. Because of my contacts with human life I have reason to know that many a soul is saying:

> "Is there anyone can help us—
> One who understands our hearts
> When the thorns of life have pierced them
> Till they bleed?"

To any such who may be listening to me now I would say that an answer to that question is to be found in the second chapter of the Book of Exodus, at the twenty-third verse: "And it came to pass in process of time that the king of Egypt died: and the children of Israel sighed by reason of the bondage, and they cried, and their cry came up unto God by reason of the bondage. And God heard their groaning, and God remembered his covenant with Abraham, with Isaac, and with Jacob. And God looked upon the children of Israel, and God had respect unto them."

How varied are the experiences through which most of us have to pass! As we reach some vantage-point, and look back over the way we have travelled, we may well thank God that the future is veiled from our sight—otherwise it would not be possible to go on.

Does God Care?

It is not only that the nights have been long and dark, but the days have been dark also, and terribly trying. Many a bitter draught we have been compelled to drink: many a severe pain we have had to endure; many a load has seemed as if it would crush so that we would never be able to stand up again—and it has not been without reason that we have sometimes wondered if God really cared!

If I could look in upon some of you this morning and have a heart-to-heart talk, it would not surprise me to learn from your own lips that the suggestion has more than once whispered its way up through your soul that God does not care—that it is too much to expect that a Creator so infinitely great should be bothered with an individual life so insignificant as you feel your life to be. Let me assure you that Satan is responsible for such a suggestion. It is his aim to get us to think that God does not really care. However, in the presence of an open Bible, we know that God both knows and cares.

Think of the history of Israel during that long exile in the land of Egypt. Don't you think that they must often have wondered whether God knew or cared? I am sure they must, even though the question might never have escaped their lips.

A wonderful promise had been given. A covenant had been entered into and solemnly attested. Yet, here they are in an alien land, slaves, when by the terms of that covenant they were to be free and in a land of their own, a land that was said to flow with milk and honey.

The Quiet Place

What is the answer in their case? It is to be found in our text: "God heard — God remembered — God looked upon — and God had respect unto." God heard their cry of anguish—God remembered His covenant with Abraham, with Isaac, and with Jacob —God looked upon Israel's sufferings in the light of that covenant—and God had respect unto the terms of that sacred bargain to which He had bound Himself by an oath to keep. And the sequel is seen in a wonderful chain of events. A child is preserved and prepared for the work of delivering this people from the place of their bondage, *because God cares*. Step by step events march on toward the time when God shall conclusively prove that He both *knows* and *cares*.

Think of a world that was in a bondage worse than that inflicted upon Israel in Egypt! After a fair trial, the verdict is, "There is none righteous, no, not one: . . . . for all have sinned and come short of the purpose for which they were created." Listen to the cry of the individual life: "O wretched man that I am, who shall deliver me?" Everywhere you have moral darkness and spiritual death. But God heard, God remembered, God looked upon, and God had respect unto! So, you have the birth at Bethlehem—the death at Calvary—the resurrection at Easter—*all because God cares!*

Now there is the offer of a wonderful salvation through faith. Salvation from the penal consequences of a broken law; salvation from the despair which frequently grips the heart in the presence of disappoint-

Does God Care?

ments and shattered hopes; salvation from the fear which often comes with loneliness and neglect; salvation from the terror which strikes the imagination when we think of that hour, which we all must meet, when we leave the seen for the unseen and go forward to face the final reckoning.

Blessed be God, He saves to the *uttermost* all who will come unto Him through Jesus Christ our Lord.

"I know my heavenly Father knows
The storms that would my way oppose;
But He can drive the clouds away,
And turn my darkness into day."

A Good Investment

In the sermon on the Mount there are some words which might easily lead the unthinking to believe that they had been addressed to the rich, but a closer examination will show that in reality they apply to every human being, whether rich or poor.

These are the words as they were spoken by Jesus: "Lay not up for yourselves treasures upon earth, where moth and rust doth corrupt, and where thieves break through and steal. But lay up for yourselves treasures in heaven, where neither moth nor rust doth corrupt and where thieves do not break through nor steal; for where your treasure is there will your heart be also."

Jesus, who knew men through and through, as He still knows them, saw that when men laid up treasures it was not only to take care of present wants but to be prepared for future needs — and that was a logical thing to do in the light of certain hopes and fears to which our humanity is heir. Therefore His words of warning and advice are not against the laying up of treasure but against laying it up in the wrong place.

Probably those who knew Paul in Corinth considered him a poor man. We do know that he laboured as a tent-maker, and his own hands supplied his daily needs. But when he is judged by spiritual standards he is seen to have been fabulously rich—as any man is rich who makes Jesus Christ his trustee.

The best investment we can make is in the cross of

Christ. To hear the thunderings of Sinai, the demands of a broken law, the clamourings of a guilty conscience, and be able to say in reply, "Jesus paid it all" is to have laid up treasure in Heaven, the value of which increases with the years. Who can adequately estimate the wealth of that person who can honestly say "I know Whom I have believed, and am persuaded that He is able to keep that which I have committed unto Him against that day?"

When a man puts his affections, his soul, and his everlasting hopes into the hands of Jesus of Nazareth, he can rest assured that when he reaches Heaven he will find his deposit safe with compound interest added! Neither moth nor thief can touch such treasure as he has laid up. He has invested in something that will never depreciate — not even if civilization itself should crumble into ruins.

Let me speak to the humblest and most obscure follower of the Saviour of men and say that, like the apostle, you too can lay up untold treasures, in the glorious spiritual results of a life that is lived in vital union with the Son of God, and of labours inspired and directed by the Spirit of God. Whatever we give up for the Master's sake increases the value of our investment in Heaven, although in making the sacrifice some may label us fools!

The trouble with many of us is that in seeking to get on in this world we steal time from God which ought to be spent in prayer and in meditating upon the Word of God. Let us get away from the folly of

The Quiet Place

eating our heart out in our hunger for popularity, because, even when we get it, it is wretchedly impoverishing, and often bitterly disappointing.

Compound interest will make many a worker in quiet places enormously wealthy in the day of final reckoning. All that a man gives up of worldly self and profit and fame and ease will stand gloriously to his credit at last.

People sometimes speak in pitying tones of "poor ministers with small salaries"—but wait till heaven's treasure chests are opened in the day of judgment and see if anyone will call that hard-working soul-winner poor! If the servant of Christ is to be judged by the numbers he has influenced God-ward, few there will be who will be richer in that day of final auditing.

"What matter if I stand alone?
I wait with joy the coming years
My heart shall reap where it hath sown,
And garner up its fruit of tears."

The Folly of Indecision

I wonder if you have ever visited the eighteenth chapter of the First Book of Kings? My regret is that time will not permit our reading it together. But take my advice and spend a little while within its borders to-day. If you will go to it in the right spirit you will find it to be one of the most interesting and enriching journeys you have ever made into the goodly land of the Word of God.

The scene presented on mount Carmel is an old picture which I would like to put in a new frame and hang on the walls of your imagination in the hope that something of its beauty would steal across the landscape of your life and give an added weight to your soul.

The incident on that mountain has a message for our own times—and I hope it may be brought home to each of us with great power this morning.

When you see Elijah in the presence of Ahab and the false prophets and listen to what is being said, it is the old story of the eternal conflict between the false and the true! When the prophet of God says to Israel: "How long halt ye between two opinions? If the Lord be God, then follow Him; but if Baal, then follow him" we read, *"And the people answered him not a word."* If ever there was a time when speech could have been golden it was then—but their shame lay in their silence and what that silence signified. *Their's was the folly of indecision.* And this is still one of the most tragic faults of mankind.

Too many of us have the peculiar knack of standing with one foot on each side of certain great questions. We are continually halting between two opinions. It may be due to a lack of moral courage, or it may be because of a lack of mental ability to grasp the important features of a given situation—whatever it is, something is responsible for an undecided attitude on the part of many men—and it always makes for failure and unhappiness.

Indecision, when looked at superficially, might not seem such a terrible thing, but it has lost battles and led to the downfall of nations. When we do nothing we often damn a situation more effectively than we would have done by making a wrong decision.

Inactivity follows indecision. We would rather do nothing than risk making a courageous decision one way or another. This is a question of the greatest importance when one considers that the issues of life, even the normal, everyday experiences, all call for a choice.

It is not saying too much to say that the average individual cannot possibly carry on the affairs of life without spiritual help to see them through, and without Divine guidance in times of crisis. There comes a time in the experience of all of us when we cannot consult with friends. It is then that we are thrown back upon God Himself. And I bear testimony to the

The Folly of Indecision

fact that I have never known a man or a woman who has relied upon God to help in the making of a great choice, make a wrong choice. The Good Shepherd never loses a sheep: and He will lead His flock in every time of perplexity. But we must come to the point in our lives where we realize that His decisions and His verdicts are always right.

Permit me to say one other thing before closing this brief message. When you have reached a decision don't waste your time and strength in looking back. Get a move on and make haste while your shoes are good!

The world is not so much interested in a man's sterling qualities as in his sticking qualities! At what pressure can he work? Is he able to keep up the pace of a high-powered machine, not only to-day and to-morrow, but every day, all the time? No matter how brilliant the start may be a man fails if he cannot continue the pace he has set. The Duke of Wellington is reported to have said after the battle of Waterloo that the British were no braver than the French, but that they were brave five minutes longer. And there you have the difference between success and failure. If you fail while the other fellow succeeds, the chances are that he is not a better man than you in any other sense than that he is good five minutes longer.

The secret of success is first making up your mind on any given question or course—then get into action and refuse to tire or be discouraged! After all it is largely a question of character. The trouble with too many of us is that we have our wishbone where our backbone ought to be.

Some of us have heard the call of the Gospel and still halt between two opinions. Christ can meet our every need, but because of a lame will we cannot make up our mind to trust Him as Lord and Saviour. In your heart of hearts this morning say: "O Lamb of God, I come."

A Greater than Solomon

In the twelfth chapter of the Gospel according to St. Matthew, we have Jesus standing in the presence of the scribes and the Pharisees and addressing them with some of the most solemn words ever uttered by One Whose speech was always unique. Having time only for a single phrase we shall content ourselves with the reading of the forty-second verse: "The Queen of the South shall rise up in the judgment with this generation and shall condemn it: for she came from the uttermost parts of the earth to hear the wisdom of Solomon; and, behold, a greater than Solomon is here."

The phrase I would have you think of at this time is, "a greater than Solomon is here."

Probably in Solomon's day people would be inclined to think that a greater than Solomon could not be. And, even now, when a near-sighted, superficial view is taken, his greatness might seem to far exceed the greatness of Jesus. When you compare his great wealth, his comfortable circumstances, the pomp and glory of his kingship, with the extreme poverty of Jesus, it is not easy for a certain type of mind to see how Jesus could be thought to be greater than Solomon.

However, this is just what Jesus Himself claims—and it is a claim that carries with it tremendous and far-reaching implications. Because, if Jesus is only

The Quiet Place

human and not Divine, as some say, His claim, when closely and carefully considered is simply an expression of conceit. But no such blasphemous charge can be sustained. Jesus of Nazareth is Son of God as well as Son of Man.

Jesus is greater than Solomon in His *words*. Never man spake as He spake. As the greatest of all Teachers, Jesus conveyed the thought of His mind to the minds and hearts of mankind by the medium of speech. When you listen to His words and weigh them in the scales of sound judgment, the words of Solomon are as dross when compared with the golden utterances of Jesus. The view of life that Jesus presents is truer and worthier than the finest description ever supplied by Solomon.

It is true that Solomon was the exponent of some high ethical standards: but mere maxims do not make for morality—nor proverbs for purity. While he had keen insight into the facts of life almost his last words are "All is vanity and vexation of spirit"—and he died a disillusioned and disappointed man.

How different it is with Jesus! He broadens the basis of sin to prove that the best of men, as well as the worst, are under its blight and condemnation. He shows that sin is not chiefly a question as between man and man but between the creature and the Creator. Then He sets up a standard of holiness which is as far above Solomon's standard as the light of the sun is above the light of a candle.

Yet, He does not thereby cast men down in despair.

He, by His words, provides a mirror to reveal to man the imperfections of the human heart. Then, in the power of that same Word, He provides a magnet to draw us to the place where we get power to produce the fruit of the Spirit—love, joy, peace, long-suffering, gentleness, goodness, faith, meekness, temperance (or self-control).

The trouble with the world at present is that such fruit is all too scarce. A blind despair has taken hold of the hearts of multitudes because for too long they have placed gold where God should have been; they have lived for the present without much, if any, thought of the future; they have been so busy trying to get a good foothold on this world that they have had neither time nor thought for the world to come. The words of men have counted for more than the Word of God—and there will be little change till men give Jesus Christ His rightful place among them.

"Judge not the Lord by feeble sense,
   But trust Him for His grace.
Behind a frowning providence,
   He hides a smiling face.

Blind unbelief is sure to err,
   And scan His work in vain;
God is His own interpreter,
   And He will make it plain."

The Ways of God with Men

If you were to cross the sea to Scotland and visit that part of the romantic little land known as "The Scott Country", you might possibly come upon the village of Nisbet. If you did, it would not take much discernment to discover that it is no longer young. From the sleepy, contented air of the place, you might very easily believe that it has not changed its appearance since the year 1600 when, within its borders, there was born one destined to become one of Scotland's most saintly sons.

Three years later, the 24th of March came in on a Saturday. That night, a horseman rode up to Holyrood Palace and announced to James the Sixth that Queen Elizabeth was dead. Two days later there came a message from the Privy Council of England to say that James had been chosen her successor. It was in this way that the King of Scots became King of England and Ireland as well.

To the student of history these happenings go to show that the history of a country, like the history of a life, is not made up of a lot of unrelated events—but that even the smallest detail plays an important part in helping to determine the destiny of either a sovereign or a subject.

I wonder how many of those who are taking part with us in morning devotions have read "Ruther-

The Ways of God with Men

ford's Letters"? If I had the means, I would bestow a copy upon every intelligent soul throughout the continent! Then I would pray that each recipient might be given a sense of appreciation of the finest collection of devotional letters to be found in all the world of literature. To steep heart and mind in such writings is to take on a culture such as can be found in no other way.

At Anworth, near the Solway Firth, Samuel Rutherford ministered for nine wonderful years, preaching Christ in all the glory and sufficiency of His redemptive work. Few men exalted the Son of God as Rutherford did. To him, Jesus Christ was the fairest of all the sons of men. Blessed be the educational system that will lead a man to dedicate his gifts and graces to the service of his fellows and the glory of God.

Exiled to Aberdeen, Rutherford was separated from the place and the people he loved as only a patriot and a prophet can love. His enemies might close his lips and prevent him from preaching to the crowds, but they could not close his life! His saintly walk and edifying conversation in private gained for him many affectionate friends who came to look upon his enforced presence among them as one of the greatest blessings God had ever sent their way.

Being human, it is possible that Samuel Rutherford sometimes fretted against his circumstances and wondered why God permitted such things to happen: but, if it had not been for this imprisonment his matchless letters would never have been written. If we could get behind the outward appearance of some of the things we so deeply deplore we should probably discover that they are blessings in disguise.

While his tongue was thus bound, and his person subjected to virtual imprisonment, his pen was free and all aglow with the touch of a live coal from the heavenly altar, so that the winged words fraught with seraphic ardour, which emanated therefrom, soon converted his humble writing-table into one of the most effective pulpits then in Christendom.

As from the prisons of pagan Rome proceeded some of Paul's weightiest epistles, providing food and drink for hungry and thirsty souls in every part of the world —as from Bunyan's "Den" in Bedford jail proceeded the most admired of allegories, which, for two centuries, has fed, cheered and refreshed myriads of God's redeemed ones in all lands—so from Rutherford's cold and icy prison house in Aberdeen, proceeded those priceless letters, glowing with celestial fire, which, with undiminished power, have rekindled and fanned the flame of a burning devotion in the breasts of multitudes. Such, and so conspicuous have always been the over-rulings of the wonder-working providence of Him, who in His own good time and way, will always destroy the wisdom of the wise, and bring to nothing the understanding of the prudent.

The most superficial study of history will convince anyone but a fool or a bigot that there is a superintending Power which takes a very real part in the affairs of men and nations. Link up your life with that superintending Power and you will be more than surprised at the difference it will make both for time and eternity.

> "With mercy and with judgment,
> My web of time He wove,
> And aye the dews of sorrow,
> Were lustered by His love.
> I'll bless the hand that guided,
> I'll bless the heart that planned,
> When throned where glory dwelleth
> In Emmanuel's land."

Journeying toward the Sunrising

With the hope that it might prove to be a helpful morsel for your mind to-day, I am going to suggest that you take as your watchword these nine words which are to be found in the eleventh verse of the twenty-first chapter of the Book of Numbers: "And they journeyed in the wilderness toward the surising."

The people are now organized to go in and possess the Promised Land. The task would not be an easy one, but that was nothing to worry about. When we get a thing for next-to-nothing it is usually worth it. They were to discover that life is neither a picnic nor a dress parade. Every step of the way toward their desired goal would be contested by forces which were out of harmony with the will of God.

As a geographical note indicating the route taken by the children of Israel the text is very interesting, but it is the allegorical aspect that I want to leave with you at this time. These nine words have a spiritual significance which ought to be of value to you as you go about your daily business.

Perhaps you have discovered long ago that, although we are journeying toward the sunrising, we are not always in the sunlight: "clouds and conflicts around us press". We are to be warriors as well as pilgrims—and often have to contend with entrenched stupidity as well as with the forces of spiritual wickedness. Have

Journeying toward the Sunrising

courage and go forward! In due season you shall reap if you faint not. The ripening process may seem slow but the harvest of ultimate success is sure.

The trouble with many people is that they have lost their way in a world that is restless and distracted because it will not conform to the teaching of Christ. We know that He can impart the secret of how to live, but we give no indication of accepting His terms. The result is that even the prosperous are often unhappy and discontented. It would be better for all of us if we put duties before rights, character before cleverness, conviction before appetites, and dull thoroughness before showy stunts.

Permit me to point out that all who would journey toward the eternal sunrising must begin that journey at the Cross of our Lord Jesus Christ.

For Israel's sin, God provided a remedy. Centuries later Jesus referred to this remedy in these words: "As Moses lifted up the serpent in the wilderness, even so must the Son of Man be lifted up: that whosoever believeth in Him should not perish but have eternal life."

The Cross stands forever between the guilty soul and all the condemnation of the broken Law. Sin's dread consequence has been averted by the sacrifice of the Son of God. The light of the Easter morn has transformed the place of death into the place of life. God's favour has displaced His frown; the garment of praise is given for the spirit of heaviness, and sobbing gives place to singing. Behind us is the radiant glory of deliverance from bondage, and ahead is the prophecy of all that is laid up for them that fear Him. We are journeying toward the sunrising.

But I must add that all who journey toward the sunrise must be prepared for the disagreeable: for the way of our pilgrimage lies through a wilderness—a wilderness that is always unkindly and dangerous.

If you take a near-sighted view of life this will seem a thing to be avoided. But you will make the mistake of your life if you do so. As the wilderness with all its discomforts was inevitable for Christ, so is it for all who would follow Him.

It was in the wilderness that Jesus hungered and was tempted to take a short cut to satisfy that hunger. Are you starting out upon this day hungering for something? To satisfy that hunger are you being tempted to resort to means that really dishonour God? Before you yield to that temptation stop for a moment to think of the purpose and power of God as set forth in the Cross. Your *greatest* need was met then! Trust Him to meet this also — and you will discover that angels are ready to come and minister unto you. Take the larger view of life and you will see that the wilderness lies toward the sunrising and the Land of Promise.

The horizon does not end with the wilderness but continues toward the sunrising, shining more and more unto the perfect day. If it ended at the wilderness what a tragedy life would be for many of us!

Journeying toward the Sunrising

Keep your face toward the sun and the shadows will all fall behind you.

> "Then let us smile when skies are gray,
> And laugh at stormy weather,
> And sing life's lonesome times away:
> So worry and the dreariest day
> Will find an end together."

The Ministry of Affliction

This morning's meditation is dedicated to suffering ones everywhere, and the text upon which it is based is to be found in Paul's Second Epistle to the Corinthians, chapter four, verses seventeen and eighteen: "For our light affliction, which is but for a moment, worketh for us a far more exceeding and eternal weight of glory; while we look not at the things which are seen, but at the things which are not seen: for the things which are seen are temporal but the things which are not seen are eternal."

The most casual reading of the context will show that the afflictions which had come upon the apostle were anything but light, as men are accustomed to weigh such things—for few have ever been called upon to suffer as he suffered; but his ability to magnify the unseen and the eternal had the virtue of making the seen and the temporal appear to be much smaller than these appear to the man of no or little faith.

Out of the most unlikely circumstances, through the medium of some sorely tried life, God often speaks to arouse and inspire a multitude of other lives. What the rest of the world owes to those who have suffered, and in their sufferings have been able to smile, will never be known in time—if, indeed, it will be known in eternity. The mere fact that suffering, or some other condition over which we have no control, shuts us up to the confines of four walls, does not necessarily mean that for the present we have exhausted the possibilities of a life of service for God and humanity. We may be shut up but we need not be silenced! Our very sufferings may give an added emphasis to the value of our influence upon others if, instead of pining, we are found praising. Prison songs have a quality all their own; and those who hear them feel strangely and strongly moved.

We may be passing through some modified Gethsemane, with the temptation strong upon us to question the goodness and wisdom of God; but if, like our Royal Master, we will sincerely say, "Not my will but Thy will be done" the testimony of our broken, imprisoned life, may be far more eloquent than any other kind of testimony man can bear.

"We live in deeds, not years;
In thoughts, not breaths;
In feelings, not in figures on a dial.
We should count time by heart throbs;
He most lives who thinks most, feels the noblest,
Acts the best."

Judged by this standard, some smugly complacent souls are going to get an awful jolt in the day of final reckoning. Many a suffering one can find an echo to these lines singing its triumphant way through a breaking heart:

"My candle burns at both ends;
It will not last the night;
But ah, my foes, and O my friends,
It gives a lovely light."

The Quiet Place

A prisoner at Rome, with the possibility of being led forth any day to pay the price of his allegiance to Jesus Christ in dying the death of a martyr, Paul—with every human reason for thinking only of himself and the making of plans for his own release from prison—seems to lose sight of his own needs in praying and planning for the needs of others.

The philosophy of his life at this time, under such trying circumstances as he was passing through, might very profitably become the philosophy of all of us. For it is a fact, which experience confirms, that the best way to help ourselves is to get busy in trying to help and encourage others. In getting under the load of some other suffering soul, your own load, in some strange way, seems to get lighter; or there comes into your back some added strength. It is out of great sufferings that great saints are made.

To be born with a silver spoon in your mouth may seem a very desirable thing, but such supposedly fortunate ones do not always prove to be the most valuable citizens or our finest Christians. All that Paul ever got or became, came as the result of hard working and sore suffering. No man ever became a saint in his sleep. It was through wakeful nights in a Roman prison, and painful days in self-sacrificing service for others that the apostle reached the grandeur and glory of his unexcelled Christian character.

In his letter to the Ephesians he speaks of himself as "the prisoner of the Lord". Rome thought he was her prisoner, but he knew that he was really the prisoner of the Lord. Paul believed that the disposal of his life lay with God and not with Caesar. It was his firm conviction that, since saving grace had pardoned him at the Cross, sovereign grace would preserve him on earth till such times as God might want him in heaven. He recognized the important part that the permissive will of God played in his life—and that all circumstances, even the most trying, only reached him after they had passed under the scrutiny of the all-seeing eye of the Omnipotent God. The man who believes in the predestinating purposes of God is simply unbeatable.

Living Life Over Again

This meditation is based on the twenty-third chapter of the Second Book of Samuel. David's fortunes are at a low ebb. He is a fugitive from the wrath of Saul. The road before him is rough, and it is skirted with a hedge of thorns which is both tall and sharp. What used to be a rose-garden is now a desolate wilderness —and where springs of water used to be, the ground is dry and thirst-provoking.

The narrative has a suggestive touch. We are told that it was "the time of harvest". The sun is hot, and not a bit of greenness is in sight. Memories crowd in upon him. In his mind's eye he can see the well at Bethlehem; and there is nothing he desires so much as a drink of its cool, refreshing water. But lying between him and that well are obstacles that he cannot surmount. What shall he do? He begins to live the past all over again. He is once more a young man shepherding sheep, and with them he has come to Bethlehem's well. He can almost hear the patter of their feet, as if it were all taking place now. He is drinking: and the more he dwells upon the past the more intense becomes his thirst, till he cries out, "Oh that one would give me to drink of the water of the well of Bethlehem."

How like something else this all is. There is a far deeper meaning to it than a cry for a drink of water. It is like the cry of the present for the return of the past. It is the man of to-day wanting to live over again the experiences of yesterday. Exile that he now is, hemmed in by forces too strong for him to overcome, he remembers how pleasant those old days were as he compares them with the present which seems to have brought nothing but sorrow and care—and he wants to escape into the past.

David is not the only one with such longings, for there is scarcely a life that has not at some time or other wanted to bring back the past. Oh, if we could begin all over again! But it cannot be! The Policeman of the Passing Years says to each of us, 'Move on!' and, whether we like it or not, we've got to obey. Nevertheless, who has not seen the children come home from school and failed to find the sentiment of these words surging through his or her soul?

"Oh, to have the clear eyes,
　The naught-in-sight-that's-drear eyes,
　The never-shed-a-tear eyes,
　That served me as a boy.
Give me back the bright eyes,
　The every-soul-is-white eyes,
　The things-must-come-out-right eyes
　That brought me only joy."

What is it but another version of the cry that was heard that summer afternoon in the long-ago, when the exile king cried, "Oh that one would give me to drink of the water of the well of Bethlehem."

The sunny skies of romantic Greece could not silence it in the soul of Byron as he gave the world words that stir the hearts of Scotsmen the world around:

"Oh for the crags that are wild and majestic,
The steep frowning glories of Dark Lochnagar."

There are times in the experience of all of us when memory goes back to the earliest scenes of life. We see the old school, and those who played with us in the rosy time of life's young days. We had no worry, and were free from all care then; and often wish now that we could go back and be as we were. Again and again we see the old church, with its memories so sacred, and its influences which have followed us down through the years. What would we not give to be able to go back and live through those days again? But it cannot be.

Could you bring back the old surroundings, you would accomplish nothing but pain and disappointment, unless you could bring back the child that moved among them. And that cannot be done.

"There's a hope for every woe,
And a balm for every pain,
But the first joys of our heart
Come never back again."

Our yesterdays are all done with till the day of judgment. Therefore, if we are wise, we shall make the most of to-day, that there may be no vain regrets to-morrow. It will always be true that every sunrise is a birthday and every sunset a time of reckoning. Take care of your beginnings in every venture in life, and you will have little cause for lamentation when you have reached the end of the way.

Living Life Over Again

'Tis not in seeking,
'Tis not in endless striving,
Thy quest is found.
Be still and listen,
Be still and drink the quiet
Of all around.

A Tonic in a Text

As a watchword for the day I suggest that you take the first verse of the twenty-seventh Psalm: "The Lord is my light and my salvation; whom shall I fear? The Lord is the strength of my life; of whom shall I be afraid?"

When you grip the meaning of that text, and its power begins to pulsate through your being, a new consciousness is going to characterize your life. Defeat is going to give way to victory! Joy will take the place of sorrow, and laughter the place of tears! Therefore, give the text a resting-place in your mind and let it simmer throughout the hours of this day, so that the Spirit of God may have a chance to play the part of a teacher — enlightening your understanding and strengthening your will.

The man who first uttered the words of our text was no fool. He had an intellect second to none. As poet, prophet, and king, he stands in the very forefront of that noble company whose greatness no wise man will challenge or dispute.

Do you ever have the feeling that something terrible is going to happen? If you do, show your good sense by getting rid of the feeling as soon as you can. Go out into the fresh air and take a walk. If you cannot do that, wash your face in cold water—the colder the better! Perhaps a good book will help you—one with a little laughter in it. Try calling up some of your friends; or, if you cannot do anything else, get up and shake yourself and start over again. *What you need is the tonic that is to be found in our text.*

Avoid, as you would avoid a plague, people who worry over every idle hour they have, thinking of the misfortune which may never come. Absent treatment is the best sort of treatment for such folks. To be much in their company, unless you go in the capacity of a doctor with the ability to help them, is to be infected with their peculiar disease.

There is trouble enough in actual experience for most of us—but why make yourself miserable till you have reason? It is foolish to use up to-day's strength in wrestling with to-morrow's burden. Trouble in the future usually seems greater than it really is — for imagination is a wonderful magnifying-glass. Most of us who have worried over troubles before they arrived have discovered that, when the circumstances have confronted us, the reality has usually been insignificant.

Make a bold bid for confidence in yourself. Go out —in the strength which the text offers—to meet and overcome all obstacles. If you do not believe in yourself, you need not be surprised if no one else will. Go ahead on the assumption that everything is going to turn out well, and see how your difficulties will fade away like mist in the sunlight. Even though the worst come, it will always be true that as your day is, so shall your strength be.

Some of our thinking needs correcting. Ask the average individual what a school is and more than likely you will be told that it is an academic building, with text books, class yells, and an encyclopedic atmosphere. If that be a full and final definition of a school all our school days would be confined to that period when we were attending such an institution. But if such be our thought we are mistaken. Our school may be an office, a workshop, a bit of farm land, a factory, a store, or a seat on a delivery waggon. We spend most of our life attending some kind of a school.

Every life needs training if it is to be lived to the greatest possible advantage. Greatness is never accidental. Genius has never been able to get along without hard work. There has never been any such thing as extemporaneous success. Moses had to spend eighty years getting ready to do forty years' work. It is the man or the woman who has been well educated in the school of experience who rides opportunity to success.

Don't allow impatience to spoil your chances. The school term may seem long, but it is necessary if you are to matriculate with something more to your credit than a piece of parchment giving you the right to add certain letters to your name! *There are no short cuts to the jobs that really count for the most.* Better to lengthen your period of education than shorten your career. Never be ashamed of your text-books. Overalls, and a kit of tools, are no humiliation to any real man. Don't waste your time and strength in envying those who have inherited wealth. The best capital is not money. It is brains, character, energy, and Christian manhood. And Christian manhood is to be had at the Cross.

A Tonic in a Text

Go out to meet the unknown experiences of the day with this song in your soul: "The Lord is my light and my salvation; whom shall I fear? The Lord is the strength of my life; of whom shall I be afraid?" And in the day of final examination you will hear the Chief Inspector say: "Well done good and faithful student—come up higher, and enter into the joy of the Lord."

"Every day is a fresh beginning,
   Listen, my soul to the glad refrain;
And, spite of old sorrow and older sinning,
   Take heart with the day and begin again."

A Singer and a Song

When I consider some of the letters which came from the hand of the Apostle Paul I can well believe that prison songs are sometimes the sweetest, and that out of the sufferings of some breaking and bleeding heart the best of good cheer is sometimes transmitted to the children of men. This is transparently true in the case of the Epistle to the Ephesians, and is all the more remarkable when we remember that it is the least personal of all Paul's letters.

Yielding to the desires of organized religion, Rome had put Paul in prison in an attempt to curb his activities and silence his testimony, little thinking that God had any particular interest in the matter, or that He would be likely to over-rule their doings to the end that they would carry out His own designs. How nearsighted most of us are where spiritual matters are concerned—and how stupid even the wisest of men are when they leave God out of their reckoning!

The time would come when the apostle would have to say farewell to all his friends in the church and take his last look at earthly scenes—but, when his presence would be withdrawn, God wanted his ministry to continue, so that while he might be dead he would still continue to speak! But how could this be unless God could enlist his pen? And how could He get the use of that pen so long as Paul was at liberty to go everywhere preaching the Word? So God, in the case of Paul's prison experiences, gives us another illustration of what is meant by making the wrath of men to praise Him. Paul's enemies meant it for harm, but God overruled it for a larger good than even the apostle's liberty could have accomplished.

When we get to know God in any vital, friendly way, we come to see that even a prison is better for us than a palace if it be according to the Divine purpose.

It is possible that there were moments in Paul's experience at this time when he began to wonder why such things as the imprisonment of an innocent man should be permitted by an All-Wise and All-Powerful God. At any rate, if he had been like most of us, that is how he would have felt and questioned. Sometimes there is no eloquence quite so impressive and overpowering as the eloquence of helplessness. And there is no language quite so convincing as the language of enforced silence.

In his salutation to the Ephesians, this is how the apostle speaks: "Paul, an apostle of Jesus Christ by the will of God, to the saints which are at Ephesus, and to the faithful in Christ Jesus; grace be to you, and peace, from God our Father, and from the Lord Jesus Christ."

Grace and peace! What a wonderful combination! The one, the cause; the other, the effect. Grace to help in every time and every kind of need! Peace to keep the heart and mind at rest and sane when all about us

The Quiet Place

is in a state of turmoil, and everybody seems to be crazy! Grace, like the blue vault of heaven above us, with its smiling sun and bracing air. Peace, like the blue depths of the ocean, so tranquil and so calm.

How can ordinary human beings, such as most of us are, enter into the enjoyment of these? Only if, like Nicodemus, we come to see the necessity of a spiritual birth, bow to the inevitable, and claim the birthright of those who have been made partakers of the Divine nature. With that settled, God in a very real and vital sense becomes your Father, and you are in a position and condition to claim all that goes with a spiritual sonship. But, be doubtful about that and you will not dare to exercise the children's privilege of claiming what you want from the Father's stores! Instead, you will miss the unmeasured blessing of an unspeakable rest which enfolds and holds the heart of the child as it draws us close to the Father's side!

Ordering our lives after this fashion, we are living as Jesus lived; and, like Him, we shall live in the perpetual possession and enjoyment of *grace* and *peace*. Let our oft upturned eyes witness to the attitude of our spirit. Let there be no film of separation, or cloud of misunderstanding between us and our Heavenly Father.

> "The happiest heart that ever beat
>   Was in some quiet breast,
> That found the common daylight sweet
>   And left to Heaven the rest."

At the Beginning of the Best

In the thirty-fourth Psalm, at the sixth verse, we read, "This poor man cried, and the Lord heard him, and saved him out of all his troubles." And in these words we are presented with a concise and complete chapter in the biography of a soul—such a biography as each of us is writing, whether we have any literary ability or not.

Here is a man, with all the hunger of heart and thirst of spirit, with all the hopes and all the fears to which man is heir—and, in addressing his Maker, his first words are in the nature of a *confession*. He confesses that he is *poor!*

Now we are not to think that he is talking in terms of gold, and bonds, and real estate. A man might have as much of these as the greediest could desire, and still be poor. There is a poverty of the spirit, a poverty of the heart, a poverty of faith, of hope, of inspiration. And there are multitudes suffering from such poverty to-day.

We are at the beginning of the best when we are conscious of the worst. We are never going to have so much as when we confess that we have nothing. We are on the eve of being blessed with every blessing of a spiritual nature in heavenly places when we can sincerely say, "Nothing in my hand I bring, simply to Thy Cross I cling."

The text says that "This poor man *cried*. That is, he did the most elemental thing in human experience.

The Quiet Place

A child can do it. There is never any need of schooling in order to know how to *cry*. And when used as in our text it constitutes the most eloquent and fruitful kind of prayer that any human being can present to God.

As in the case of the Psalmist, it is indicative of a state of helplessness. This man has got to an end of himself because he has reached the end of his resources. It is when we reach that position and condition that God usually gets a chance to begin on our behalf. It is only when there is taken out from under us the things on which we have been accustomed to lean, that we are disposed to lean upon God. Only when the foundations of our faith in the sacraments get shaken by the thunderings of Sinai are we ready to build upon the Rock of Ages. We have to be stripped of all the garments of self-righteousness, in which many of us are clothed, before God gets a chance to wrap around us the robe of Christ's spotless righteousness.

This cry betokens *earnestness*. This is one of the greatest needs of the religious life of our day. We are so cold, so calculating, so correct that we are more like a creation in marble than human beings made of flesh and blood. We lack the spontaneity of the early Christians. Even though we sing lustily, "Fight the good fight of faith," the sort of fighting we engage in is more like a sham battle than real war. We are never going to spend more time in prayer unless we are going to be more in earnest.

No soul ever *cried* to God without being heard.

At the Beginning of the Best

There is always deliverance to be had by those who feel their need and cry unto God in sincerity and in truth. God delights to *save*. He never fails to save those who, in simplicity of faith, earnestness of purpose and consciousness of need, call upon Him in the time of trouble.

But what kind of deliverance do you want? You may be delivered *out of* all your trouble—or you may be delivered *in* your trouble! To be delivered out of trouble will always be pleasant to the flesh—but to be delivered in trouble is a greater tribute to the one who has cried!

Paul cried three times to have something taken out of his life which he described as "a thorn in the flesh", but, to all his crying, God made answer, "My grace is sufficient for thee." And Paul finally reached the place where he could say that he would rather glory in trouble that the grace of God might be magnified in him. If a single chapter out of your spiritual biography could be revealed what kind of a story would be told?

"I gazed on the throng of hurrying faces,
Some in tatters and some in laces,
And I said to myself, "How will it be,
When the soul of each is at last set free?"

The Technique of Living

His words came to me like the lament of a lost soul: "The truth is I have failed altogether to acquire the technique of living. Man is born to be happy, but my happiness has always been just around the corner. Man was born to be free and is everywhere in chains. I have forged my own chains, built my own cage round about me, and beat my wings like an imprisoned peregrine because I can no longer soar."

What a confession of human failure! Yet, mark you, the man is reckoned a success by all who think they know him. He is cultured, clever, prosperous! But I fancy he has discovered that what is commonly counted success is superficial and transitory. It is not easy to reason men into such an attitude to life! Experience alone can teach some people.

What a commentary on the culture of our civilization! Hungry for happiness, yet compelled to starve. Born to be free, yet all the time in chains—confined to cages built by ourselves. Although it is the confession of an individual soul, it is equally true of the universal heart. Out of Christ, none can honestly say that he has acquired the technique of living.

Man is a sinner by nature and by practice. He sins in thought, in word, and in deed. If he were a perfect personality he would be perpetually happy and free—morally and spiritually.

The stream of human life must have started somewhere. This stream is polluted. There may be many contributing causes since—but an original cause must be found to explain how the pollution started. The explanations given by some philosophers may be clever but they are not convincing. Some modern scientists say that sin is due to the conflict of the ape and a higher reason evolved by slow degrees. But I prefer to accept the Word of God when it says in effect what has been said elsewhere: "Sin is any want of conformity unto or trangression of the Law of God."

We are driven back to the Federal Head of the Human Race to find the cause of all human failure. In Adam all die — only in Christ shall all be made spiritually alive. Christ saves us from the penalty of sin by His Cross, and offers us the technique of living in the warm light of the Easter morning.

One grey day, when snowflakes were in the air and the ground was somewhat soft underfoot, a day when there was not much cheer about unless one happened to have it within one's own soul, I watched and listened to a man who seemed to have acquired the technique of living.

When I saw him he was working under conditions that would have tried the patience of a gilded saint. He had turned his coal cart into a private driveway only to have the wheels mire deeply. His one horse could not budge the load of coal. He coaxed the horse and shoved at the wheels but there was "nothing doing". He scratched his head, pulled his horse's ears playfully, scolded it in a good-humoured way—*and then he began to sing!* All the while he kept on working, pausing in his song occasionally to reproach the striving horse with sarcastic humour. At last he gave up the effort to move the cart and began to unload his coal at that point, carrying it some distance to a basement opening.

As I watched him without his knowledge, I could not help wondering how many men could have conducted themselves as well under similar circumstances. Some drivers would have scorched the atmosphere with oaths, while brutally beating the horse. How much better was this man's way. Instead of helping the situation, cursing and cruelty would have only done further injury to his own soul, and been a proof that he had failed to acquire the technique of living.

It is a rare spirit which can smile and sing under stress and provocation. Wise is the man, or woman, and happy as well, who can look out and up and at the exasperating things in life, and all the while keep singing. The man at the coal cart made the grey morning appear bright with the radiant glory of self-conquest.

Christ's first word after His resurrection, and His last just before His ascension was "*Peace*". It is the portion of those who have discovered the technique of living. The blessedness of such a life is not in the absence of loss or sorrow, but in the assurance of the unchanging presence of Him Who ascended to the right hand of the Majesty on High, there to act as our advocate until such times as He shall come forth—Prince of Peace—to reign as King of kings.

"There are loyal hearts, there are spirits brave,
There are souls that are pure and true;
Then give to the world the best you have
And the best will come to you."

Love's Triumphs

"I may speak with the tongues of men and of angels, but if I have no love, I am a noisy gong or a clanging cymbal:

I may prophesy, fathom all mysteries and secret lore, I may have such absolute faith that I can move hills from their place, but if I have no love, I count for nothing.

I may distribute all I possess in charity, I may give up my body to be burnt, but if I have no love, I make nothing of it.

Love is very patient, very kind. Love knows no jealousy: love makes no parade, gives itself no airs, is never rude, never selfish, never irritated, never resentful; love is never glad when others go wrong, love is gladdened by goodness, always slow to expose, always eager to believe the best, always hopeful, always patient." (Moffatt.)

The greatest transforming agency in all human experience is love. Let us cultivate its closer acquaintance and we shall be surprised at the difference it will make. When a man chose to believe the devil's lie rather than God's truth, and the poison of sin entered human experience, it was love that heard the cry of human need and gave the promise that the seed of the woman would bruise the head of the serpent, and make salvation from sin and its awful consequences gloriously possible for mankind.

Many centuries later, it was Love that selected Heaven's finest choristers and sent them forth to sing o'er the star-lit hills and plains of Bethlehem of the fulfilment of that ancient promise in the birth of the child, Jesus. And, in the place selected for that birth, Love showed its power to transform the humblest surroundings into a veritable holy of holies.

In the unique life that followed that birth, we have Love in action. In His presence, the skin of the leper becomes like that of a little child; blind eyes leave the darkness of an awful imprisonment for the light of a glorious deliverance; ears that have never heard a sound are enabled to hear the faintest whisper of the Divine voice. As the embodiment of Love He projects a word into the silence of the tomb, and the cold, still ear of death responds in resurrection of life and loveliness.

It was Love's supreme sacrifice when He gave Himself a willing substitute for sinners, and, in their place, died on the cross of Calvary. Then there came an hour when the warmth of that Love melted the iciness of our unbelieving hearts and brought us in surrender to His claims as we sang:

> "O Love that wilt not let me go,
>   I rest my weary soul in Thee;
>   I give Thee back the life I owe,
>   That in Thine ocean depth its flow,
>   May richer, fuller be."

In that surrender we experienced the expulsive power of a new affection—and now, "As we climb the

The Quiet Place

hill of Christian experience, and gaze into the ever-growing horizon of the ocean of Divine tenderness, we become ashamed even to mention the pool of our love, which lies far away in the vale beneath—besides we come to see that all true love is but a reflected gleam of His great love, we love Him because He first loved us."

> "I am only a child who is lying
>   On the bosom of infinite Love.
> I speak not of living or dying;
> I know not of sorrow or crying;
>   My thoughts are dwelling above.
>
> All I need without price I am buying
>   By my trust in the Goodness above.
> There's an end to my yearning and sighing,
> For just like a child I am lying
>   On the bosom of infinite Love."

Wasted Privileges

In the twenty-sixth chapter of the Gospel according to St. Matthew, at the thirtieth verse, we read, "And when they had sung an hymn, they went out into the mount of Olives."

Here it was that Jesus uttered those great words which are to be found in chapters fifteen, sixteen, and seventeen of the Gospel according to St. John: and I can think of no better investment of our time than to read through these three chapters several times at one sitting, just as we would read a news report in some newspaper. Don't pause to ponder any particular text until you have made this experiment, and I will guarantee that you will get something of the greatest possible interest and value which otherwise you might miss. Indeed, I believe that it would add greatly to our culture if we had the patience and were willing to take the pains to commit these three wonderful chapters to memory. What a privilege to be with Jesus in the Upper Room, and to go from there with Him to the mount of Olives and the garden of Gethsemane! The olive was the emblem of peace: and there, in the garden, knelt One, in infinite agony, Who is "Our Peace".

Do we realize how highly privileged we are in being permitted to be near when He is pouring out His heart to the Father? Let us pray for wisdom to make the most of it.

The Quiet Place

Sometime previous to this hour Peter had refused to admit the possibility of failure. Others might forsake the Master and deny Him, but Peter would remain loyal to the end. It was simply unthinkable that he would ever prove false to his Lord! Yet, despite his profession of superiority to the others, Peter made a poor use of his privilege. He slept when he ought to have been supplicating. And in his failure at this time he paved the way for his failure later.

Try to imagine, if you can, what he must have missed seeing and feeling when he failed to watch with Jesus for "one little hour". If we can spell victory upon our knees we shall never know defeat elsewhere. There are some things that can only be done by prayer and fasting—and to attempt them otherwise is only to be disappointed in disaster.

Think of Christ's teaching about prayer! Some of the most wonderful words ever uttered were uttered by Jesus on the subject of prayer.

Think also of the example He had set! Early morning—and He is at prayer. Late night—and again He is at prayer. Surely, if anyone could have lived and laboured without prayer it would have been Jesus! And if He could not—do you think you can?

Peter had been present on almost every occasion that Jesus was speaking about prayer—yet, see how little he had profited by what he had heard and seen. If Peter's wits had not been wool-gathering when Jesus was teaching or illustrating in His own life the art of prayer, he would, when Jesus warned him of impending failure, have prayed most earnestly to be delivered from defeat. But he neglected prayer—followed afar off—and ended by denying the Lord when he ought to have defended His cause and witnessed to the Saviour's power to save and satisfy the deepest desires of the soul.

How often it is so with the professing Christian; and that in spite of the teaching of God's Word. We gather at the Communion Table with others and with the risen Christ; we partake of the bread and the wine: we blend our voices in song—*then*, out into a world, that is at the best unsympathetic, we go, to forsake Christ in the hour of trial and to deny Him when we ought to glory in the opportunity presented, to confess Him as our Lord and Master.

Think of the history of the Church, and think of your own personal experience, and tell me if any of us can afford to find fault with Peter.

One reason why sin and the world make such havoc of our lives is just because we fail to make the most of the Upper Room. When the communion chamber is allowed to make the contribution it is capable of making we shall come to know how wonderful it is to watch with Him "one little hour".

It is in the Upper Room that we are able to get above the dust and din of this materialistic age. It is here that we can see how small and mean and selfish the world often is. It is in the Upper Room that we see how hypocritical religious leaders can sometimes be. Here it is that we learn why the Church is often

The Quiet Place

so powerless, and why there is a dearth of conversions. Motives are tested here as they are tested nowhere else. Here you will get courage for the long dark night of loneliness, and have a finer appreciation of the value of human sympathy. Here you will feel the touch of a friend's hand—catch the look of a loving eye and be strengthened by the tones of a voice of trust and loyalty.

"When I am very weary
I do not try to pray.
I only shut my eyes and wait
To hear what God will say.
Such rest it is to wait for Him
As comes no other way."

Working Toward Success

Am I speaking to someone to-day who feels that his life is being lived on too low a level? Does the position you occupy fail to satisfy you? Are you ambitious for something better than you have yet attained? Do you believe that there is a niche somewhere which will never be filled until you take possession of it? Are you chafing under your limitations, and longing for that larger opportunity which will enable you to express yourself in some more adequate way? Then permit me to say that the man who said "Hitch your waggon to a star" knew something about both the philosophy and the psychology of life—and his advice is well worth taking to heart and putting into practice. For it is the man or the woman who has some definite aim who will eventually rise above the common level.

Do you know anything of an experience which would make it quite pertinent to say to you, "if ye then be risen with Christ, seek those things which are above?" If not—why not? When Jesus said to Nicodemus that what he needed was a spiritual birth, He was really speaking with equal force to every other human being. And in stating that fact He was presenting the one supreme factor in all real success.

When a man has an aptitude for business, coupled with a burning desire for great wealth, nine times out of ten such a man will amass a comfortable fortune, even though he may never reach the larger goal for which he strives. The same is true of any man, statesman, author, doctor, lawyer, preacher, artisan—or whatever he may be—who desires to travel just a little beyond the average, and who keeps his eye on the path he wishes to pursue. Unswerving loyalty to an aim in life will get any man farther toward success than will riches for most men who have inherited them.

If I am speaking to some man who is "up against it" and, feeling as blue as can be, is ready to throw up his hands in despair, permit me to remind you that while circumstances of birth, and sometimes misfortune, may check a man's progress—many men, despite such hindrances, have mounted high on the ladder of what the world would call real success. Spurgeon was right when he said that some men owe the very grandeur of their lives to the tremendous difficulties which they have had to overcome.

Halted though you may be on your journey, keep your face toward the light while you trudge on to your goal. Even though at the end of the road you discover that the object of your aim in life still lies beyond your reach, you will have the satisfaction of knowing that you have travelled farther than you would have done, had it not been for that insatiate and impelling force that kept you toiling on to reach the top of the hill. It is my belief that every worthy ambition which has not been realized in this life will be realized in that still more wonderful life which lies just beyond the present order of things.

It is foolish to talk as some have done about "The Key to Success" when every intelligent person ought to know that success is not under lock and key. It is something that can neither be patented nor copyrighted. Success has always been a matter of hard work, and it can never be anything else. Whatever short-cuts there may be in this world, there is none to success. Go over the list of really successful men today and you will not find an idler among the number. I believe that it is impossible to find a single man or woman who can be considered successful who has not worked long and hard and patiently. Get close enough to any musician who has become famous and you will discover that he began early, that he worked day and night to perfect himself in his art, that he never ceased working—and that while his admiring and applauding audiences are asleep after his performance, he is hard at work. Don't fool yourself in thinking that there is a key to success, and that all you have to do is find the key and success will come your way with speed and ease. Success is not locked up. Anybody can reach it if he is willing and ready to work hard.

Jesus says to each of us, "Follow me, and I will make you." To follow is not to drift but to drive—not to dream but to do! No man ever became a success in his sleep! You must awake and get to work early and be willing to stay late if, at the end of the road, you are to hear Him say, "Well done, good and faithful servant." Take your eyes off the clock and fix them on Christ and see what a difference it will make.

"The fault, dear Brutus, is not in our stars,
But in ourselves, that we are underlings."

Wanted—More Reality

Nearly three hundred years ago, Bishop Hall gave utterance to a lament which many of us could quite fittingly make our own. This was the burden of it: "If God had not said, 'Blessed are those that hunger' I know not what could keep weak Christians from sinking in despair. Many times, all I can do is to complain that I want Him, and wish to recover Him."

These words bear a striking resemblance to a cry that fell from the lips of Job,—"Oh that I knew where I might find Him! that I might come to His seat. I would order my cause before Him, and fill my mouth with arguments." You will find it in the twenty-third chapter of the book that bears his name. To me it is like the cry of a man who has got tired of playing the game of make-believe in religion, and now refuses to be satisfied with anything but reality.

I wonder if any of those who are listening to me this morning feel disposed to disagree with me when I say that the life of the average church member is more conspicuous for its consciousness of the *absence* of God than for a sense of His *nearness?* Is it not a fact with many of us that, even when the forms of worship and devotion are observed conscientiously, the consciousness of the Presence of the Invisible God, with the joy that a sense of His nearness brings, is by no means with us?

Take the matter of prayer. Is it not true that there are hours in our devotional life when we are all too painfully conscious of the absence of reality? We speak—and our speech is orthodox—we have the devotional dialect, but it is all so superficial. It makes as little impression upon us as the music does upon our radio. We have no words which are, as George Herbert says, *Heart deep*. We experience no ecstasy, no joy, no peace, no repose. We have no sense of being at home with God. The stillness of The Quiet Place is too often just like the stillness of a dead calm at sea. True, we have thoughts of God, of Christ, of eternity, of heaven—but our heart rocks monotonously on the surface of it all:

"As idle as a painted ship
Upon a painted ocean."

Yet I am confident that this is not as God would have it. I know from His Word, and from the experience of certain great souls, that something far different is possible for all of us.

I read that Jesus took Peter and John and James, and went up into a mountain to pray. And as He prayed, "the fashion of his countenance was altered." I am sure that something similar will happen in our experience when we really begin to pray. The reason why the fashion of our countenance is not altered is just because there is so much unreality in our prayer life. If we would be wise enough to let Jesus work out His will in us, He would take us up into the mount of communion and prayer to show us what is possible in the life of the most ordinary piece of humanity when it falls into line with the Divine purpose.

To read the life-story of some men who were made of the same sort of clay as ourselves is like taking a tonic for the soul. We are told of Payson that his mind, at times, almost lost its sense of the external world, in the ineffable thoughts of God's glory which rolled like a sea of light around him at the throne of grace.

In the case of some, so overpowering was the revelation of God which opened upon their souls, that they recoiled from the intolerable joy as from a pain, and besought God to withhold further manifestations of His glory.

Jonathan Edwards tells us of the sweet hours which he enjoyed on the banks of the Hudson River in secret converse with God. What God has done for others He is willing and waiting to do for us.

What we need is just to have one experience when we feel the relish, and are enticed by the deliciousness, refreshed with the comforts, made acquainted with the secrets of real prayer, and we'll never be satisfied with anything else again.

> "Prayer is the simplest form of speech
> That infant lips can try.
> Prayer is the sublimest strains that reach
> The Majesty on high."

Devotion to a Purpose

Writing from the inside of a Roman prison, with the shadow of death falling across his heart and his hopes, the greatest of all the apostles refuses to be discouraged. From that hour when the risen Redeemer met him on one of the world's chief highways, to bring the proud Pharisee into vital union with Himself, Paul had manifested a devotion to a great purpose such as has never been excelled if, indeed, it has ever been equalled.

Despite his unprecedented sufferings he refuses to change the key-note of his life. But from his prison we can hear the convinction of his soul give a clarion-like quality to his voice as, exultingly, he cries, "For to me to live is Christ, and to die is gain." Then he bears testimony to a fact we are in danger of forgetting—namely, that the development of character need not be stopped or stunted, although the body is locked up behind prison walls of stone and mortar, or behind walls of physical weakness and bodily suffering. If history shows anything, it shows that some of the greatest sufferers have become the greatest saints.

Listen to him, as out from his place of confinement, he sends this testimony to the Church at Philippi: "Brethren, I count not myself to have apprehended; but this one thing I do, forgetting those things which are behind, and reaching forth unto those things which are before, I press toward the mark for the prize of the high calling of God in Christ Jesus."

If we are not advancing we are falling back. There

is no such thing as standing still on this side of death. If we are not keeping alive, growing to something better and higher, we are becoming weaker and of less worth. We should have something to work for, and work for it. Whatever it is, let it be something of more than passing value. It is not wise to live just for the fleeting moment. Without some aim one's time and work go for naught. The years go by and there is nothing to show for them. Have some worth-while aim toward which you are all the time travelling. Even though you never reach the goal, you will make some real advance in striving for it. It will always be true that a good aim, a real purpose in life, makes for worth of character. The one universal aim should be to live truer, better lives, from day to day.

It may be all right to be content with what we have, but it can never be right to be content with what we are. Cromwell said, "If I cease to become better I shall soon cease to be good." The language of Paul should be the language of us all. His were not the words of one who was nothing more than a bundle of emotions. There has never been a keener intellect, nor a more logical, than was possessed by the man who, in that statement from the Epistle to the Philippians, shows the trend of his thought in the consecration of his whole being to a great progressive purpose.

A life without a purpose has been likened to a ship without a rudder. It is true, whether we believe it or not, that aimless cutting produces nothing but chips, whether it be a block of marble or a human life. Want of motive makes life dreary and monotonous. Nothing satisfies! Better little talent and much purpose than much talent and little purpose. If you want to be something more than a very ordinary piece of humanity you must have an uplifting ideal. Such an ideal will play the part of wings to your soul, and will set your mind and body on fire with eagerness for the thing you want to do. Aim for something worthwhile and keep your aim steadily in view. Life will then mean much more to you. You will then not only be more useful in the world, but you will also find more satisfaction in living. Remember that where you may be to-morrow depends very largely upon the road you are taking to-day.

"Chisel in hand stood a sculptor boy
  With his marble block before him,
And his eye lit up with a gleam of joy
  When his life dream passed before him.

He carved it well on the shapeless stone
  With many a sharp incision;
That angel dream he made his own,
  His own that angel vision.

Sculptors of life are we as we stand
  With our souls uncarved before us,
Waiting the time when at God's command
  Our life dream shall pass o'er us.

If we carve it well on the shapeless stone,
  With many a sharp incision,
That angel dream we make our own,
  Our own that angel vision."

The Ministry of the Mountain-Top

In the seventeenth chapter of the Gospel according to St. Matthew, we are told that Jesus took Peter, James and John, his brother, and brought them up into a high mountain apart and was transfigured before them. This is always what happens when Jesus gets the leadership of a life. It may be the life of an ancient Galilean fisherman, or the life of some modern mechanic or merchant prince, but it starts on the upward path of real progress and lasting prosperity when it comes under the influence of Jesus.

If you would enjoy the inspiration of an ever-widening horizon you must put yourself under the convoy of Christ and He will lead you to the spiritual uplands, where you will make the discovery that those who live there can neither age nor die.

For the moment you may be far away in some vale below, getting little of the sunlight and finding life dull and uninteresting—but you would gladly exchange the gloom of the valley for the glory of the sun-kissed mountain peaks if you only knew how to get there!

It is written, not only in the pages of the Word of God but into every fibre of our spiritual make-up that "the path of the just is as the shining light that shineth more and more unto the perfect day." Put your trust in Him Who is "the Way, the Truth, and the Life" and you will at the same time exchange the grey and

and the mists of the lowlands for the sunlight and the joy of the uplands.

It is unfortunately true that many of us live dull, grey, languid, commonplace lives, knowing practically nothing of higher spiritual experiences. Such is the tragedy of unbelief—a tragedy that might be turned into triumph if we had faith as a grain of mustard seed.

The life of most of us needs to be more satisfying than it often is. We need to give ourselves to something bigger and greater. The life of the most ordinary human can be greatly enriched and made far more satisfying if we will let the Son of God take us apart into some mount of transfiguration. The mountain-top enables us to replace new enthusiasms for the stale round of meaningless activities which so often characterize our lives. In the clear light of that choice spot there is to be found new nourishment and stimulation for empty and hungry lives.

On the mountain-top, in the company of Christ, you are put in the way of learning some valuable lessons which cannot be learned in any other way. Standing in the presence of Jesus as He explains the past and relates it to the present and the future, you come to see that the one sure way to be saved from a narrow outlook and straitened sympathies is to take full advantage of the mental and spiritual breathing spaces which the mountain-top provides. While we linger there, there comes to us the determination to understand this world of ours, and to develop our capacities to the fullest, so that our lives will widen in scope and meaning.

The Quiet Place

Some people live so much of their lives on low levels that it would take a mental derrick to lift their minds out of the deep ruts of conventionality into which they sometimes settle. The mountain-top will do this; and at the same time give a spiritual vacuum cleaning that will freshen the whole of our inner furnishings.

On the mount of transfiguration the Bible becomes a new Book. The old dispensation is brought up-to-date; and spiritual forces are both seen and felt. Here you come to see that while the Book may undergo new interpretations its authority is not altered or affected by time. All that is required is to approach it with an open heart. While it will doubtless set before you your shortcomings, and make you feel your limitations, it will at the same time open up before you a way out of all your difficulties. If you look upon Jesus as the incarnation of the Divine thought as that thought affects humanity in time—past, present and future—you will find satisfaction in the revelation, no matter from what angle you may approach it.

It is on the mount of transfiguration that you meet real religion, and experience the freedom such religion always brings. The mountain-top will release your energies, expand your horizons, enlarge the range of your activities and bring you into creative and expansive moods.

Nothing ever gets done without faith enough to release energy. We need a faith that will pick us up, put us on our feet, dust us off, and start us on our way again. The mountain-top will give you this.

Some people imagine that the opposite of faith is reason—but they are very much mistaken in so thinking. Nobody has any right to have an unreasonable faith. The real opposite of faith is cynicism and fear. These freeze life, but on the mountain-top a faith is begotten that thaws out the coldest life and sets it free to accomplish its finest achievements.

> " 'Downward the path of life!' Oh, no!
> Up, up, with patient steps, I go;
> I watch the skies fast brightening there;
> I breathe a sweeter, purer air."

Meeting the Unexpected

In the fourth chapter of the Gospel according to St. John, we hear the interesting story of Jesus and the Samaritan woman as they met at Jacob's well.

In the course of the conversation which followed, Jesus said to her: "If thou knewest the gift of God, and Who it is that saith to thee, Give me to drink, thou wouldest have asked Him, and He would have given thee living water."

Like the woman of Samaria, we often stumble, quite unexpectedly, on some of life's greatest moments. It would be well if we remembered that many of life's largest opportunities wear the garments of the ordinary, and at first sight are apt to be mistaken for the common-place.

Jesus said, "*If thou knewest*". The trouble with many of us is that, as we travel along life's dusty way, we fail to realize the marvellous opportunity with which we are faced when we meet Jesus. If we knew all that is made possible in contact and communion with Him we should seek the sense of His presence more than anything else. He offers to put into our soiled hands wealth such as our wildest dreams never imagined possible. He speaks the word that stills the fitful fever of our aching hearts, and brings a message of salvation and courage and hope.

"If thou only knewest" the dangers and the difficulties and the burdens that are ahead of you; the dark lonely places where the presence of a friend will make all the difference between victory and defeat, between deliverance and despair, you would appreciate above all else the friendship and abiding companionship of Jesus.

None but Jesus would ever have expected any radical change in this woman. No other seemed capable of discovering a hungry heart underneath a cheap and tarnished dress. Man looketh on the outward appearance, but God looketh upon the heart. Jesus knows the handicap which is sometimes imposed by heredity and environment, and is always ready to make full allowance for all our failures, not holding these things against us, but making it possible for us to experience the expulsive power of a new affection, and giving with it the promise of brighter and better days.

How true it is, and how blessed also, that we never can tell what a day will bring forth. To people of vision and imagination this adds a still greater charm to the art of living. Rob human life of its sense of mystery and you bring it down to the level of the beasts of the field. The man of good sense and spiritual discernment finds it easy and exhilarating to believe that every morning is a birthday.

It is the break of day! Lying behind us is the darkness of the night covering the mistakes of the previous day, even as the blood of His cross covers the multitude of our sins. A new beginning lies before us as we go forth to meet the unknown quantity in life. What it may hold of bitter or sweet, of pleasure or pain, of success or failure, only God can tell.

Testings are sure to be met, because such are necessary for the development of character. You may come suddenly upon the seemingly impossible. If you do, remember that Lord Kelvin said that, when we are up against an impossibility, we are on the edge of a discovery.

To reach the place of perfect satisfaction and realize the Divine purpose in human experience, we often have to face the disagreeable—but I still think it is true that he is not worthy of the honeycomb who shuns the hive because the bees have stings! The way to health of soul, as well as the way to health of body, often holds some bitter medicine for us. Keep this in mind and it may help you over many a rough bit of road.

If I were starting life to-day, enlightened somewhat by what I have already learned, my earnest prayer would be, "O Lord, give me sense to see that the best investment in the world is to be found in serviceable, awakening, stimulating education; the development of a keen, lively, exploring mind, and a disinterested curiosity about life. Help me to be moderate in the use of all things except fresh air and sunshine."

When we feel our weakness and contemplate our ignorance, would it not be well, ere setting out to meet the day's experiences, to put ourselves intelligently and unreservedly under the watch-care of a loving Heavenly Father?

If you have had the good fortune to have met Christ, pray for a deeper reverence, a clearer and more comprehensive vision, and a wholesome enjoyment of the fact that, when you are up against a seeming impossibility, you are on the edge of what may turn out to be the most wonderful discovery you have ever made.

"If you were born to honour, show it now:
If put upon you, make the judgment good
That thought you worthy of it."

Losing One's Ideal

In the twenty-first chapter of the Gospel according to St. John, from verses three to six, you will find these words: "Simon Peter saith unto them, I go a fishing. They say unto him, we also go with thee. They went forth, and entered into a ship immediately; and that night they caught nothing. But when the morning was now come, Jesus stood on the shore: but the disciples knew not that it was Jesus. Then Jesus said unto them, Children, have ye any meat? They answered, No. And He said unto them, Cast the net on the right side of the ship, and ye shall find. They cast therefore, and now they were not able to draw it for the multitude of fishes."

The history of mankind is very largely the history of man's search for the ideal.

A worthy ideal is the worthiest thing a man can have. If we would know a man's true wealth we must consider, not his material possessions, but the measure of noble aspiration which stirs his being. The man of noble ideals is the richest man on earth, even when he has to be buried in a borrowed grave.

Worthy ideals redeem life from the merely ordinary, while the want of them degrades a man and leaves him a clod or a clown. God's true knight is lured on by ideals. When he crosses his Euphrates it is in quest of the city which hath foundations, the city whose

Losing One's Ideal

maker and builder is God. The light that shines not on sea or shore lights his way—and onward he goes "o'er moor and fen" with a song of everlasting joy in his heart, for he hath beheld the image of the man he would like to be. Henceforth, life for him is one grand and sometimes fierce effort to transmute the dreams born in him by the Divine breath into the warp and woof of daily life.

It has been said that the man of noble ideals is the most homeless man on earth. The foxes have holes, and the birds have nests, but the idealist hath not where to lay his head.

We have heard men say that the home of the fox knows no change; its dawn was also its zenith! But witness the landscape of man's life: a thousand homes has he built for himself, and a thousand homes hath he left desolate. For no sooner is the roof completed on his latest house than his ideal lures him on to something different and better. He never seems to be able to reach his limit. In his alphabet there seems to be no Omega. No matter how great his grasp it always is exceeded by his reach. Resting-place on earth hath he none, for his reach is even unto the heavens.

The man of noble ideals creates, enriches, transforms. He is the saviour of the nation to which he belongs. Homer created the ideal that saved his land. Christ saves the world by revealing Himself as the ideal Man, Redeemer, and King.

Our text suggests that Peter had lost his ideal. His

The Quiet Place

harp hangs mute upon the wall. The zest has gone out of his life.

His experience of Jesus, when he first met Him, had given him his ideal. The death of Jesus had deprived him of it. To him the cross was the tragedy which had shattered all his hopes. Then he returned to his old life, his boat and his nets. He tried to resume that life where it was before Jesus had called him, but he made the discovery that after Christ touches a life no one can lapse into the old life as if nothing had happened. At this point in his history Peter discovered that a lost ideal will haunt us as long as we live.

When he returned to his former manner of living he found everything the same except himself. His years with Jesus had left their mark on him. Though he had lost his ideal he could not forget it. He soon found out that he could not run his enlarged life into the old forms. He had outgrown them!

"That night he caught nothing." In some strange way his hand had lost its cunning for that sort of thing. For him the old life had lost both its meaning and its music. As he trod the sands of the sea of Tiberias he seemed to be treading them with feet of lead. He did what many are doing to-day—he looked for food amid the ruins of an obsolete experience—but found only husks.

Then morning came—and with it came Jesus!

It is always the dawn of a new day when Jesus puts in an appearance. He waits on the shores of our shattered hopes to restore us our lost ideals.

Losing One's Ideal

O aching heart, out there somewhere, amid the ills and wreckage of life, a healing force is at work. Jesus comes to lead us from defeat and unrest to victory and peace.

"Every day is a fresh beginning,
  Listen, my soul, to the glad refrain;
And, spite of old sorrow and older sinning,
  Take heart with the day and begin again."

Why These Denials?

In the First Book of Chronicles, at the second and third verses of the twenty-eighth chapter, you will find David standing in the presence of a great company of the leaders in Israel, to whom he is reviewing his past life, laying special emphasis upon one experience which at first both pained and perplexed him. As that experience had certain elements in it which might be in any of our lives, I am going to use it as the basis for this meditation.

These are the words as you may find them in the text: "Then David the king stood up upon his feet, and said, Hear me, my brethren, and my people: As for me, I had in mine heart to build an house of rest for the ark of the covenant of the Lord, and for the footstool of our God, and had made ready for the building: But God said unto me, Thou shalt not build an house for my name, because thou hast been a man of war, and hast shed blood."

Ever since their wilderness wanderings, the Tabernacle had been identified with the life of the Hebrew people. Within its precincts the Shekinah Glory, symbol of the Presence of the Invisible God, could be seen above the mercy seat.

None had a deeper love for the House of God than David. Everything about it was dear to his heart. Its faded curtains, stained with the travel and wear of the years, seemed to be interwoven into every fibre of his imagination. For long years he had desired to erect a suitable and more permanent place of abode for the ark of the covenant: but, for some reason that was not given at first, he was not permitted to perform what his heart had purposed. And the glory of David in that hour was that he did not rebel against the Divine refusal, but meekly accepted it as necessary for his own good and the glory of God.

I wonder if we, with far greater spiritual advantages than David had, can be as submissive to the Will of God when it runs flatly in the face of our own feelings? Remember, we have what David never had—we have the New Testament with the light it sheds upon much that used to be dark and inexplicable. In the light of that fact we have less excuse than he had. We have good reason for questioning the reality of our religious experience if we cannot bow in humility to the Divine refusal—believing that since God knows best, it would be folly on our part to try and force any other course. It is a question whether we have got any faith if we are not willing to trust where we cannot trace.

Despite the disappointment which the denial at first brought, David's life was all the richer for having been so sensitive to the impulse of a noble purpose. I am quite sure that there came into his life an added strength as he graciously accepted the will of God as the one safe course for him to follow.

I wonder if there are those listening to me this morning who are wondering why an All-Wise Providence does not permit or enable them to realize some ideal that they have in life. You love the beautiful, but you have to accept the unlovely. Some dream of music haunts you through all the hours of the day as its rich harmony clings to your soul. Yet all around you it is mostly discord. Work, you have no heart for—drab surroundings, uncongenial company—these constitute your lot in life; and you are both perplexed and pained at the workings of Providence when you are denied the one and compelled to face the other.

Believe me, there is a reason, and a good one too, for God's unwillingness to help you do here and now the things you desire to do—even though, as in the case of David, He does not at first explain the reason for the refusal. As He did with Israel's king, so He does with you: He smiles, I think, as He says: "It is well that it is in thine heart." Your life is the richer, your horizon the wider, your vision the clearer for having had the desire; and you will have achieved a great victory when you can sincerely say, "Thy will be done."

God's denials are sometimes very delicately delivered; and at first He speaks His "No" very gently. The bruised reed He will not break, and the smoking flax He will not quench. If, for some reason best known to Himself, He is not prepared to respond to our cry and remove the thorn in the flesh, He will not fail to say, "My grace is sufficient." He honours our intelligence and challenges our faith by leaving us to infer that there must be a very good reason why our request is refused.

Why These Denials?

"So I will trudge with heart elate,
And feet with courage shod,
For that which men call chance and fate
Is the handiwork of God."

A Startling Question

The question to which I refer came to me from the the pages of a magazine, and, at first sight, I must admit, it seemed to be somewhat crude. But at least it had what many a more polished phrase lacks—it had the virtue of being arresting. It laid hold of my imagination, and started me off searching in the hope that I might find an answer to this question: "What is God driving at?"

In my quest I made the discovery that the world divides itself into two classes. In the first place there are those for whom life is just an existence. It may often be a glittering existence, with the glitter being mistaken for the gold of something worth-while, but in it there is not much thought of God or of the future. It is a case of living mostly for self and the present. They are alive intellectually—alive physically—but, in the language of the New Testament, they are dead spiritually. They have no vital relation to the Giver of all spiritual life.

In the second place, there are those for whom life is an experience. To them, God is real—God is near and tremendously interested. God's Word is their delight. In the study of it, they come to see that God has a plan for every life; and, to carry this plan to a successful consummation is what God is driving at. "For whom He did foreknow, He also did predestinate to be conformed to the image of His Son."

A Startling Question

This, then, is the purpose of God: *conformity to the image of Jesus Christ*. The Cross has this as its objective. It is not merely a case of "getting us off", it is a case of making us like Christ.

We are to be like Him in *character* and in *conduct*. And there is no surplus of either within the Christian Church to-day. If the purpose of God were realized in the experience of those who claim to be the recipients of His redeeming and regenerating grace we should be less liable to hear men say, "Well, if that's Christianity, I don't want it." There is no greater stumbling-block to the reception of the Gospel than the inconsistency of professing Christians.

Conformity to the Divine Image is the object of all God's dealings with us. Nothing happens by chance! Behind all life's experiences, there is a Head that has planned; a Heart that loves; and a Hand that guides.

"Back of the loaf the snowy flour,
Back of the flour the mill,
Back of the mill, the wheat and the shower
And the sun, and the Father's will."

"And we know that all things work together for good to them that love God, to them who are the called according to His purpose." All things are not necessarily good, nor does the text say that all things are good. But there is a superintending power which causes all things — the bitter and the sweet — the pleasant and the painful — the dark and the bright — the cruel and the kind, to work together for good.

How different life becomes when you recognise

The Quiet Place

this! A story is told of a gentleman who visited a deaf and dumb institution, the superintendent of which told him that Providence seemed to compensate the children under his care for the handicap imposed in their deaf and dumb condition. "Take a piece of chalk, and question them, and you will discover that they are unusually bright," said the superintendent.

The gentlemen went up to the blackboard and wrote this question: "Can any of you children tell me why you are both deaf and dumb while I can both speak and hear?"

At a sign from the superintendent that anyone was at liberty to write the answer if he felt able, a young lad walked up to the blackboard and wrote this answer: "Even so, Father, for so it seemeth good in Thy sight."

What a different day this might be if we went out to meet all that it holds for us in the strength of such an attitude as is reflected in this story!

Likeness to Christ in character and in conduct is the desire of every true soul. With some it becomes a passion; and the world speaks of them as *mystics*. Can't you sense the intensity of Paul's desire for realization of this in his own life when he says: "That I may know Him, and the power of His resurrection, and the fellowship of His sufferings, being made conformable unto His death; if by any means I might attain unto the resurrection of the dead. Not as though I had already attained, either were already perfect: but I follow after, if that I may apprehend that for which also I am apprehended of Christ Jesus." It is not a normal

Christian life where this desire is not to be found.

When a life is lived in the atmosphere of prayer—under the influence of the Holy Spirit—and sustained by the Word of God, the key-note of such a life is expressed in these lines:

> "Jesus, let me seek for nought,
> But that Thou should'st live in me,
> Let this only fill my thought,
> How I may grow like Thee."

And, last of all, it is the assured outcome of all life's experiences.

Knowing our hearts as we know them, it sometimes seems hard to believe that the image of Christ can ever be developed in us. We are so prone to wander and to err! By-paths of sin have a stronger attraction for some of us than the paths of righteousness and peace. It is so easy to doubt, and so difficult to believe, that we often despair of ourselves; and marvel that God can have patience with us. Nevertheless it is written in the Word of God, and written into the very texture of the divine life within us, that the Divine Purpose for each of us whose faith is in the Cross shall be gloriously realized at last. "It doth not yet appear what we shall be: but we know that when He shall appear we shall be like Him, for we shall see Him as He is." "For whom He did foreknow, He also did predestinate to be conformed to the image of His Son." Better things are lying ahead of us than the best we have yet known.

Praying Women

Wherever the Gospel has penetrated, women have been quick to respond to its call; and have given themselves unreservedly to promote its interests, even to the uttermost parts of the earth. Throughout the world they are observing this day as a day of prayer—and it is to such women that we are dedicating this meditation.

After Jesus left His disciples and ascended to take His place at the right hand of the Majesty on high, His followers returned to Jerusalem and sought the seclusion of a well-known trysting-place — there to wait upon God for the fulfilment of a promise which would provide them with all needed power for the carrying forward of the greatest mission ever committed to the care of mankind.

In the first chapter of the Acts of the Apostles we read, " And when they were come in, they went up into an upper room, where abode both Peter, and James, and John, and Andrew, Philip, and Thomas, Bartholomew, and Matthew, James the son of Alphaeus, and Simon Zelotes, and Judas the brother of James. These all continued with one accord in prayer and supplication, *with the women, and Mary the mother of Jesus,* and with His brethren."

Sometime previous to this, Jesus had said, "Again I say unto you, if two of you shall agree on earth as touching anything they shall ask, it shall be done for them of my Father which is in heaven."

It is possible to use these words without knowing anything about their actual meaning. I don't believe that one of the disciples understood the first thing about the philosophy of prayer. Probably they had not the faintest idea as to why it should be necessary for the creature to plead with the Creator for anything that was really necessary for the good of mankind or for the glory of God. I can not get away from the feeling that if they had given the subject of prayer an intellectual analysis they might very probably have ended in a state of agnosticism.

As rational beings we have some very decided limitations: and, because of these limitations, there are certain questions, regarding which, if we are to get anywhere, it must be by the exercise of faith rather than by any enlightenment which comes from a process of reasoning. In the realm of prayer the just shall live by faith.

Success in prayer is not determined by intellectual comprehension, but by childlike simplicity of trust and the surrender of our moral nature to those invisible forces which God is always waiting to let loose on our behalf.

No pledge has ever been given by God which He will not in His own good time redeem: and He has never raised a hope within the human heart to dash it to the ground of disappointment and leave us in a state of despair.

Your power in prayer is not determined by the extent of your understanding of the philosophy of it, but by your willingness to take God at His word, your readiness to trust where you cannot trace, and by a great longing in your heart to see the will of God done in the earth.

There was never a time in the memory of any of us when difficulties were so many and so great: but these very difficulties are a challenge to vital Christianity, and a test of the reality of the faith we profess to have. *I know that prayer makes a difference at the other end.* I know it because God's Word proclaims it, and because I have proved it in my own experience.

One glorious antidote for the ills of life is the ministry of intercession. Prayer is a pleasant path to tranquillity of mind. O troubled soul—wherever you may be to-day, amid the crowded city or in some quiet hamlet, on land or sea, at home or abroad; no matter where—God's ear is open to the cry of the worst as well as the best of mankind! God has appointed prayer as a means to the attainment of peace. Prayer lifts the soul above the cares and vicissitudes of life. By the magic of its ministry you get nearness to God.

Turn to Psalm one hundred and second and meditate upon its opening words till their majesty compels you to bow in awe and you begin to feel yourself carried along in their might: "Hear my prayer, O Lord, and let my cry come unto Thee. Hide not Thy face from me in the day when I am in trouble; incline Thine ear unto me: in the day when I call answer me speedily."

When you think of it you can easily see that the most elemental thing in human experience is *a cry*. No schooling is needed to learn how to do it; and I believe it to be the most eloquent prayer ever presented by the creature to the Creator.

"Approach, my soul, the mercy-seat,
　Where Jesus answers prayer:
There humbly fall before His feet,
　For none can perish there."

Guided by God

At a certain moment in time, and in a way that left David in no doubt, God said to him: "I will instruct thee and teach thee in the way which thou shalt go: I will guide thee with mine eye. Be ye not as the horse, or as the mule, which have no understanding: whose mouth must be held in with bit and bridle. . . ."

What a glorious promise to come from the Creator to the creature! It is a promise that applies with equal force to all who have trusted Christ for salvation. It has wonderful possibilities for every life that will put it to the test. Sit down quietly, with your Bible open at the Thirty-Second Psalm, and ponder it until the significance of it grips your imagination.

We believe that we have every right to call God "Our Father". As sinners, we have been to the Cross and claimed the shelter and saving efficacy of that all-sufficient sacrifice. And, on the basis of that act of faith, we have experienced a spiritual birth, by virtue of which we have been made sons and daughters of the Most High. It should therefore be natural for us to look to our Heavenly Father for guidance in all that pertains to our life and work.

I suppose that most of us have had our days when we have dreamed of success. Perhaps we have tried to command it by calling to our aid various kinds of

Guided by God

expedients, only to meet with disappointment and be left at last feeling ashamed and disheartened.

The question, then, is: "How can I know the way in which God would have me walk, and the work He would have me take up?"

Now, because there is so much at stake, the importance of this question cannot be exaggerated. It may mean either the enlargement or the limitation of our power to *be* and to *do*—and it may also be the determining factor in the measure of peace that possesses our souls.

Ever since man was turned out of the Garden of Eden, God has never failed to guide those who have had the courage to trust Him to the limit—trusting Him sometimes when reason has been inclined to rebel and faith has been made to look foolish.

Perhaps one of the most magnificent exhibitions of faith is to be found in the case of Abraham when he left kindred and country and started out across the trackless desert to reach a land of which he knew practically nothing. But he believed that he was in line with the will of God; and for him it was enough to rest in the fact that God knew what was at the other end of his venture of faith.

Those who are acquainted with the New Testament know how the members of the early church were enabled to thread their way through the most perplexing problems of ways and means—laying down principles which will guide the Church until her mission on earth is done—and all because of their dependence upon the Spirit of God.

God's gracious assurance to all who have received the grace of spiritual discernment is, "I will instruct thee and teach thee in the way which thou shalt go." How comforting it is to have God say to us, "In all thy ways acknowledge ME and I shall direct (or make plain) thy paths."

When we are where God wants us to be, we are in the place of plenty. The clouds may refuse to give rain, the crops may languish and die, while the whole landscape looks barren and uninviting. There may be evidences of famine on every hand—but God will see to it that our needs are met, even if He has to commission a few ravens to do it. He never sends any of His people forth at their own charge. He meets all expenses when they move at His bidding. When they put themselves under His watch-care He assures them that even in the wilderness He will see that they do not lack any good thing. He has a Pillar of Cloud for the day, and a Pillar of Fire for the darkness of the night. There will be manna on the desert sand—springs in the wilderness—honey in the rock—and the soul shall be clothed in raiment more wonderful than the lily, to walk in that hour when the desert has been turned into a veritable rose-garden.

God usually guides us in one or other of three ways; and sometimes in all three at once! By an *impression* within our hearts: by His *Word* reaching us from without; and by His *Providence* around us. When all three focus into one point you no longer doubt, but believe — no longer delay, but act; and in doing so prove that the steps of a good man are ordered by the Lord.

As one of the greatest of the prophets says: "The Lord shall guide thee continually." O trembling soul, you may look to Him for guidance through all your life with its myriad necessities, and you will never be disappointed. The great thing in the world is not so much where we stand, as in what direction we are moving.

"He leadeth me: O blessed thought!
O words with heavenly comfort fraught!
Whate'er I do, where'er I be,
Still 'tis God's hand that leadeth me."

Sinning and Suffering

If you were to open your Bible at the twenty-first chapter of the Second Book of Samuel, you would find these words: "Then there was a famine in the days of David three years, year after year." And if you know anything of Palestine you will have no difficulty in realizing that a famine in that land created a serious condition for all concerned. It was always the result of the failure of the winter rains. Such a failure was by no means uncommon, but in this case it came in three successive years. Therefore it became alarming. It compelled both sovereign and subjects to think seriously. And there is always hope when you can get people to think. Probably as much harm is done by want of thought as is done by wrong thinking. It is when a man begins to think of his ways that he turns his feet unto the paths of righteousness and peace.

Then we read, "and David enquired of the Lord." Confronted with a problem that he could not solve—bowed down beneath a load too heavy for him to carry—depressed by a darkness too dense for the eyes of his understanding, he did the only logical thing left for him to do: he "enquired of the Lord". He now acts on the principle that it is better to know the worst in the light of the Lord than to grope after the best in the dark.

It was a great pity that he did not do this in the first year of famine: he might have prevented two-

Sinning and Suffering

thirds of the suffering. There is something of real heroism in the man who is not afraid to go into the presence of God to seek the interpretation of that which is obviously a Divine visitation.

The ultimate cause of God's displeasure might be in himself! David knew his own heart too well to dismiss that from the realm of the possible. Nevertheless he wants to know the truth since it is the truth that makes men free. He reasoned that such a national disaster as famine in three successive years could mean only that God had an unsettled controversy with His people. As long as this is so, there will be trouble.

The cause of all the trouble was sin: and sin always entails suffering, not only for the guilty but often for the innocent. O to have nothing in the life but what is well-pleasing to God! What a different day this might be for all of us if such were the case for each of us!

To David's enquiry as to the cause of this strange visitation, it is written, "And the Lord answered, it is for Saul." Then follows the indictment in detail. Kings count for something as between subject and sovereign, but not as between the creature and the Creator. God is no respecter of persons. Despite the fact that David was God's Anointed, and is called "the man after God's own heart", the famine was in the days of David.

This is a warning to the best of men—and glorious encouragement to the worst of us.

The Quiet Place

The life of faith is at its best when it turns to God in every period of perplexity. The pity is that we are so slow to believe this and to put it into practice.

"And the king called the Gibeonites, and said unto them, What shall I do for you? And wherewith shall I make the atonement, that ye may bless the inheritance of the Lord?"

How prone we are to lean upon the arm of flesh! How easy it is to persuade ourselves that it is easier to walk by sight than by faith! There was a law to which he should have appealed: and if the Word of God had been his guiding star it was to this law he would have turned instead of going to the Gibeonites. Don't let us be too harsh in our judgment, because this very day we may be guilty of the same fault ourselves.

This incident in the history of God's ancient people goes to show that all true life is of His planning, and no area or interest is unrelated to His concern. If we can really grasp the significance of such a statement, it is going to make a world of difference to us. When we recognize this, we shall enquire of Him in days of darkness and doubt—days such as we are passing through now—with the certainty that no mystery whose elucidation is necessary to our peace and spiritual prosperity will be left unsolved.

Such a life will never give way to despair: and it will never permit itself to think that somehow things have got out of God's control. But it will turn to

Him as His own interpreter of every dark or disagreeable thing.

> "When the sun of joy is hidden
> And the sky is overcast,
> Just remember light is coming
> And a storm can never last.

After a Fortieth Birthday

To those who have imagination and faith, one of the most fascinating things about prayer is that you can never tell what wonders are going to come out of it. If, sometime to-day, you would take a copy of the Word of God and sit down quietly before the record as set forth in the Acts of the Apostles, your praying powers would be both challenged and stimulated.

When Peter and John went up to the temple at the hour of prayer, little did they dream what the outcome of that prayer-pilgrimage would be. Lying across their path was a case of need which made a tremendous appeal to their sympathy, and sent surging through their souls the life-giving breath of supplication.

Here was a man who asked for *lucre* and what he needed was *life*. It was not silver and gold that he needed most, but strength and grace. Lame from his birth, he seemed to have had no ambition for anything higher than the life of a beggar. But when he met two men of God who knew the power of prayer in their own experience, he discovered himself to be on the edge of the most wonderful life imaginable.

I wonder if we have yet understood all that is implied in these words: "The man was above forty years old on whom this miracle of healing was shewed!" Had this man despaired of ever being anything different? Had he seen nothing better before him than the life of a beggar? Did his friends see nothing better ahead of him than the sort of life he had lived for so many years? Perhaps you too have said to yourself, "What can be looked for from a life that has run more than forty years of its course?"

Such a question can only arise within a heart that is pessimistic. The facts of life clearly show that many of life's greatest accomplishments lie beyond a fortieth birthday.

One, whose authority is beyond all doubt, has said: "It is well known that the most efficient and productive years of the life of a business or professional man are after he passes forty."

The late Sir W. Robertson Nicoll once said: "At no point of his life should a man despair. At any point of his life the best of his days may be before him."

"The man was above forty years old on whom this miracle of healing was shewed." And for him the best of life came after that miracle of healing.

Bunyan wrote the *Pilgrim's Progress* when he was fifty years of age. *Robinson Crusoe* was written when the author was fifty-eight. *Paradise Lost* was written when Milton was fifty-seven. The Waverley Novels were written when Scott was well over forty. *The Scarlet Letter* was written when Hawthorne was nearer fifty than forty. *Faust* was completed when the writer was eighty-two. *The Canterbury Tales* were written when the author was sixty. Dryden published his best poems when he was eighty years of age. Washington Irving was writing delightfully at seventy-five. Oliver Wendell Holmes declared that he was young at eighty-three. The world's greatest picture, "The Last Supper" was painted when the artist was seventy-seven. And it is a well known fact that Michael Angelo went to Rome to learn something when he was eighty years of age. General Booth toured Africa on a great soul-winning campaign at the tender age of eighty-one. John Wesley was at the height of his eloquence and usefulness when he was eighty-eight. Gladstone was made Prime Minister for the fourth time when he was eighty-three; and when he died at eighty-nine, none considered him old. Lyman Abbott at eighty-six was editor of "The Outlook". Robert Browning was nearly eighty when he wrote:

> Grow old along with me!
> The best is yet to be,

The last of life, for which the first was made:

> Our times are in His hand
> Who saith "A whole I planned,

Youth shows but half; trust God: see all nor be afraid!"

The fact is, a man has not arrived at his full powers at forty. Many of the world's most distinguished men did not succeed till after forty. Professor Dorland tells us that only four per cent of the world's greatest work has been accomplished before the age of forty; ten per cent between sixty and seventy; twenty-one per cent between seventy and eighty; and six per cent between eighty and ninety. All of which compares most favourably with four per cent before forty. If youth takes away some things, maturity brings other treasures that time alone can give.

The auditor of a great international concern has had a survey of ten thousand employees for twenty years, and he tells us that "A man well past fifty who knows his job is worth four times more than a young fellow on the job. He ought to be paid four times more—one fourth for knowing his job, and the other three-fourths for his acquaintance with life and his knowledge of human nature. I cannot spare the man over fifty—he is too valuable to lose."

When a life is lived in daily contact with God, each added year is but a step nearer the state of perpetual youth. Life often has its narrow places, but there is always a bit of blue sky above. And, however dark the night may be, the stars of hope forever shine.

"Ah, great it is to believe the dream
As we stand in youth by the starry stream;
But a greater thing is to fight life through,
And say at the end, 'The dream is true!'"

A Mind in Subjection

In the fourth chapter of that remarkable letter which the apostle Paul wrote to the church in the city of Philippi we read some of the most striking words to be found in the New Testament: "Be careful for nothing; but in everything by prayer and supplication with thanksgiving let your requests be made known unto God. And the peace of God which passeth all understanding, shall keep your hearts and minds through Christ Jesus. Finally, brethren, whatsoever things are true, whatsoever things are honest, whatsoever things are just, whatsoever things are pure, whatsoever things are lovely, whatsoever things are of good report; if there be any virtue, and if there be any praise, think on these things."

These words were addressed to ordinary individuals like ourselves, and what was expected of them is also expected of us. For long they had carried the consciousness of sin in their hearts, and with that sense of sin there had come fear at the thought of impending judgment. Then there had come to them the story of the Cross; and in that Cross they had been led to see God's answer to the demands of a broken law— His provision for the needs of human nature—the ground upon which a Holy God could be just at the same time that He justified the transgressor who dared to trust the Divine promise and made the great experiment, which is reflected in the words of the Psalmist when, with exultation, he cries, "O taste and see that the Lord is good: blessed is the man that trusteth in Him."

In this passage from the Epistle to the Philippians we have a picture of a mind that is stayed upon Jehovah, and so is at rest with itself. Then there is a very fine distinction drawn between prayer and supplication, with a suggestion of the part these should play in the life of one who has been redeemed from the ruinous effects of sin—with the place that thanksgiving occupies in the experience of one who submits the smallest details of his life to the will of God. The mention is made of a peace that passeth all understanding which God has provided as a garrison for the heart to hold it against every conceivable kind of enemy, not as directed by human ingenuity but as dominated by the risen Christ. From that point he proceeds to show the power of thought as the governing principle in producing a life that is true, honest, just, pure, and lovely.

In the light of this graphic description of a life that is well pleasing to God and appealing to men, many a professedly Christian life falls far short of being Christian in the New Testament sense. Any life that claims to have its source in Christ, if it is not beautiful, has good reason to fear that it may be mistaken in thinking that it is Christian after all. If our religion does not make the life lovely to look upon and pleasant to live with I am afraid that it is not the religion of Jesus Christ we have got.

The Quiet Place

It is splendid to have that strength of purpose that gives force of character, but there is no reason why that strength cannot be rugged and, at the same time be beautiful. Truth, honesty, justice, and right are important elements in a genuine Christian life—but it does not add to the virtue either of these qualities or of the person who holds them when they are not attractively beautiful. There is no good reason why any sturdy quality of character should be wanting in beauty. The homeliest virtue may be clothed in the attractive garments of grace. In order to be true we do not need to be sour or surly. A truly Christian life should have all the strength of the Rock of Ages, with the beauty and fragrance of the Rose of Sharon and the Lily of the Valley. Christ, who is always to be our model, was "altogether lovely".

Some things are not lovely but come dangerously near being ugly. There are people whose personality is anything but attractive—there is nothing of the magnet in their make-up. They neither make close friends nor keep any kind of friends. No one could charge them with anything really wrong, yet they are not lovable in their disposition. There is something about them that hinders their popularity, mars their influence, and limits their usefulness.

May the beauty of the Lord our God be upon us and express itself in meekness of spirit, humility of heart, winsomeness of disposition, a faith that removes mountains, a hope that refuses to be dimmed, and a confidence in the wisdom and goodness of God that will not be shaken though all the powers of darkness assail it.

> "The world seemed empty, and black, and cold,
> And wretched, and helpless, and very old.
> God gave me a thought; a new world grew,
> The thought created the world anew."

Seeing Jesus

There are three words in the second chapter of the Epistle to the Hebrews which give me my text at this time: they are, "We see Jesus." And I would say, first of all, that however familiar we are with the contents of the Old Testament—however well informed we may be as to its history—however capable we may be of appreciating its poetry—however gifted in interpreting its prophecies, we miss the most important thing in it unless *we see Jesus*.

Just as at one time in the world's history all roads led to Rome, so now all Scripture within the bounds of the Old Testament leads to Jesus. He is the centre and the circumference of its contents. See Him in its pages and it becomes the most wonderful writing of ancient times. As you approach it from time to time —and I hope you approach it often—come with the prayer of certain Greeks who, more than nineteen hundred years ago, said, "We would see Jesus."

"We would see Jesus, for the shadows lengthen
    Across this little landscape of our life;
We would see Jesus, our weak faith to strengthen
    For the last weariness, the final strife.

"We would see Jesus, the great Rock foundation,
    Whereon our feet were set by sovereign grace;
Not life, nor death, with all their agitation,
    Can thence remove us, if we see His face."

When we enter the precincts of the New Testament, we see Jesus in four wonderful portraits. In Matthew, He is the King. In Mark, He is the Servant. In Luke, He is the Son of Man. While in John, He is God Incarnate; and is set forth as the Way, the Truth, and the Life.

In the Acts of the Apostles, the whole burden of their preaching is to bring men to *see Jesus*. The Epistles, in their teaching, always endeavour to enable the minds and hearts of believers to *see Jesus*. In the last book in the New Testament we have "the Revelation of Jesus Christ". We see Him as the faithful witness, and the first begotten of the dead, the prince of the kings of the earth. He is presented as the One Who loved us and loosed us from our sins by the power of His own precious blood. We see Him as the Lion of the tribe of Judah, the Root of David. He is standing in the midst of the throne as a Lamb that had been slain but was now alive for evermore.

In glad anticipation we see Him by faith revealed from heaven with His mighty angels. We see Him in flaming fire taking vengeance on them that know not God, and that obey not the gospel of our Lord Jesus Christ. . . . when He shall come to be glorified in His saints, and to be admired in all them that believe in that day. Everywhere, it is Jesus!

> "Jesus only is our message,
> Jesus all-in-all we sing,
> Jesus only is our Saviour,
> Glorious Lord and Coming King."

The Quiet Place

As a sinner, have you seen Him as your Saviour? The very best of us can have no other; and thank God He stands ready to save and receive the worst.

Listen while an unknown Christian speaks and see how his speech strikes you:

"Here is a man who was born in an obscure village, the child of a peasant woman. He grew up in another obscure village. He worked in a carpenter shop until He was thirty, and then for three years He was an itinerant preacher. He never wrote a book. He never held an office. He never owned a home. He never had a family. He never went to college.... He never travelled two hundred miles from the place where He was born. He never did one of the things that usually accompany greatness. He had no credentials but Himself.

"While still a young man, the tide of popular opinion turned against Him. His friends ran away. One of them denied Him. He was turned over to His enemies. He went through the mockery of a trial. He was nailed upon a cross between two thieves. His executioners gambled for the only piece of property He had while He was dying, and that was His coat. When He was dead He was taken down and laid in a borrowed grave through the pity of a friend. Nineteen wide centuries have come and gone and to-day He is the centrepiece of the human race and the leader of the column of progress. I am far within the mark when I say that all the armies that ever marched, and all the navies that ever were built, and all the parliaments that ever sat, and all the kings that ever reigned, put together, have not affected the life of man upon the earth as powerfully as has that One Solitary Life."

"The name of Jesus is so sweet,
I love its music to repeat,
It makes my joys full and complete,
The precious name of Jesus."

James Fitzpatrick